MW00475489

TOOLKIT *for* SPIRITUAL GROWTH

*A Practical Guide
to Prayer, Fasting, and Almsgiving*

Fr. Evan Armatas

ANCIENT FAITH PUBLISHING
CHESTERTON, INDIANA

Toolkit for Spiritual Growth: A Practical Guide to Prayer, Fasting, and Almsgiving
Copyright ©2020 Evan Armatas

Published by:
    Ancient Faith Publishing
    A Division of Ancient Faith Ministries
    P.O. Box 748
    Chesterton, IN 46304

Unless otherwise noted, Scripture quotations are taken from the New King James Version, © 1979, 1980, 1982 by Thomas Nelson, Inc. Used by permission.

ISBN: 978-1-944967-81-9

Library of Congress Control Number: 2020942160

Printed in the United States of America

25 24 23 22 21 20   18 17 16 15 14 13 12 11 10 9 8 7 6 5 4 3 2

Contents

Dedication & Acknowledgments

A S IS TRUE for most authors, there are many who have helped in the creation of this book. First, I'd like to thank my wife and children for all they have taught me, and for their constant love and support. I'd also like to thank the parishioners I've served who have journeyed with me; my parents, siblings, relatives, mentors, and friends who have shaped my heart, especially Yiayia Dora and Father Tom; John Maddex for seeing something in me I didn't; and everyone at Ancient Faith. And a special thanks to Greg Drobny—this book wouldn't have happened without you.

Dad, you love books, so this first one is for you.

Introduction

WRITING A BOOK on the three spiritual disciplines of prayer, fasting, and almsgiving is a daunting task. You may know that Christ Himself taught on these disciplines in the Sermon on the Mount, which is found in Matthew 5–7. At other times during His life and ministry our Lord taught or demonstrated by example their importance and centrality.

In my role as a parish priest, I am often called on to share a word or two myself from the teaching the Church inherited from Christ and the apostles on what some call the "three-legged stool" of spiritual life. These legs—prayer, fasting, and almsgiving (charity)—together provide a stable base from which we can grow in Christ. My hope with this small book is to provide others with the same practical and simple direction I offer in person, which I pray will assist them also in their pursuit of God.

Now any member of the Church can tell you that each of the topics covered in this small book could easily take up several volumes. In fact, many writings of the saints, the Fathers, and others cover these subjects in much greater depth and detail. Their holy writings are inspired and move beyond anything one can expect here. So the question arises, Why offer another book on them?

The answer lies not in the hope of covering new territory or providing new insight but rather in my experience of being a priest in a community. What is needed to get started is often something basic. A way in, if you will, to the spiritual life that can be read by anyone. It is my hope to provide a guide to these basic and primary disciplines of Orthodox spirituality. My experience has taught me that whether you are new to the Church or you grew up in it, the basics must be understood.

In what follows it is important to understand that Christ's teaching on prayer, fasting, and almsgiving forms the basis for our spiritual life as Christians. These three disciplines lead to our transformation, and they are the basis for the life of the believing community, the Church. Everything else we do in this life and in the Church that leads to eternal life is built on them.

It is also important that the reader understand

that when practiced over time and with love, these spiritual disciplines liberate us. They free us from a disfigured way of life, what we would commonly call sin. Sin not in the sense of "doing something deserving punishment," but sin as something that defaces the image of God in us.

It is essential to affirm our belief that Jesus is the perfect man, the One who lived without sin. His life was a perfect human life, a life that was not in any way disfigured by sin. Through His life He refashioned humanity, restoring human beings to our original beauty. It was His obedience of prayer, fasting, and almsgiving (love for others in action), that led to our renewal.

Through these disciplines He opened for us a path that frees us from the disordered way of life that has become normal for many, even though their hearts and minds tell them otherwise. These spiritual practices put us back together in a rightly ordered way and lead us into life. For many such a concept seems impossible. How can a disciplined and obedient life be a free one as well? I think the simplest answer to the question is the one Jesus gave: "Come and see."

CHAPTER ONE

Prayer

"And when you pray ..." (Matthew 6:5)

Nott LONG AGO, a young man came to my parish after reading extensively about the Orthodox Church. Having grown up in a Christian home, he was seeking answers that no one in his community could give, and after reading numerous books and articles, he ended up in my office.

Within a short span of time, it became apparent that he had already read most of the books I would recommend. He did not lack understanding in basic church history or theology, but something still bothered him.

"How do I pray?" I remember him asking. For all his knowledge, he felt lost when it came to what should be one of the most basic aspects of Christian living. He told me that his prayers amounted to sitting by himself in his room and offering a stream of consciousness in his head or under his breath, because that was all he had been taught.

If that method is not, as he intuitively knew, the true, Christian model for prayer, what is? That is the topic we must address, as it is fundamental to our lives in Christ.

What follows is a rudimentary explanation of prayer. It is by no means extensive or insightful. For a much deeper and fuller treatment of prayer, the sober-minded Christian must turn to the writings of the Fathers and saints of the Church. Here we are addressing only the beginning components of prayer in the hopes of gaining a mere foothold in this way of life. Readers are encouraged to move beyond this simple work.

Prayer Is Liturgical

OUR MODERN CONTEXT has allowed many people to form some decidedly bad habits in their view of prayer, so it is important to realign ourselves with the truth. In some cases, doing so requires us to wipe the slate clean—to begin fresh by forgetting what we know (or what we think we know) and moving forward from there.

Most people are molded by self-direction and pride, which permeate every level of society and even invade a great many of our churches. This self-direction can be found in a solely charismatic method of prayer—the routine of no routine, offering up what is on our mind at any given moment. This method is so pervasive that it is all most people outside of Orthodoxy think of when the concept of prayer comes to mind.

But in the prayer life of the Church, we do not need to invent or grope; instead, we are encouraged to return to what the Church has received from God and taught since her inception. From the very beginning, the Church had a notion of how we should pray and an understanding that prayer is liturgical in nature. The word *liturgy* is a biblical one, meaning "the work of the people." By using this word in conjunction with prayer, we are suggesting that prayer is a type of work—something a Christian does and even becomes. This work does not earn salvation, but it requires the concentration of one's heart, effort, and discipline.

In the Epistle to the Hebrews, Christ is referred to as "a priest forever" (Heb. 7:17). The idea that He could be a priest but not serve liturgically would have been unthinkable to those who wrote Scripture, given their background and community. Furthermore, He is called not only a priest but a *liturgist*: "a Minister of the sanctuary and of the true tabernacle which the Lord erected" (Heb. 8:2). *Minister* in Greek is *leitourgos*, "liturgist." Worship on earth mirrors the worship of Christ, who is a heavenly priest serving in a liturgical fashion.

We can see even more direct evidence of this understanding of liturgy in the Gospels. When the disciples asked the Lord how to pray, He answered by offering what is now known as the Lord's Prayer. Christ did not respond by telling His disciples to pray whatever came to mind. Instead, He gave them a prescribed prayer, understood for centuries by the Church to be both formal and liturgical in nature. (This does not mean the prayer is not personal and direct. The point is that when asked, "How do we pray?" Jesus answered with a prayer.)

Consider the fact that there are two versions of the Lord's Prayer: one in the Gospel of Matthew and one in the Gospel of Luke. Which one does everyone know by heart, and why? It is the one in Matthew. This may be because the Matthew version is the form of the Lord's Prayer used by the people of the early Church and today, recited during the common prayer service known as the Divine Liturgy.

Take another example from the Book of Acts. In chapter 2 we read that the first community of believers "continued steadfastly in the apostles' doctrine and fellowship, in the breaking of bread, and in prayers" (Acts 2:42). Most English translations leave out the article "the" before "prayers." This unfortunately lessens the impact of what St. Luke is reporting to us. The earliest followers of Christ continued steadfastly in *the* prayers of the Church, that is, in liturgical prayer. They were literally reading set prayers. Another example occurs later, in Acts 10, which describes both Cornelius and St. Peter praying at specific times—one at the ninth hour (3 PM) and the other at the sixth hour (noon). Both of these traditional times for prayer are kept in the liturgical office of the Prayer of the Hours.

Even our earliest historical sources indicate a liturgical life of the Church. The *Didache*, one of the oldest Christian manuscripts in existence, gives a requirement for how often we say the Our Father. Believers in the early Church never expected an individual to invent his or her own prayers and routine for prayer discipline based on feelings of the moment; they understood prayer in the context of the life of the Church body. Prayer was done within the rhythm and method of the Church.

So we must return to the basis of prayer as the Church has given it to us. What has she taught? Before we answer this question, we should note that a liturgical understanding of prayer does not imply that we must completely put away extemporaneous and emotional prayer; rather, we must move this style of prayer out of its position of primacy. We must keep it in its proper role and context so that it does not result in our prayer becoming self-serving and self-directed. To put it another way, extemporaneous prayer cannot be our principal method, as we cannot enter the Church without repentance, humility, and obedience. This means we put aside a personal search for what prayer looks like and receive the Church's teaching.

Adam and Eve, You and Me

To UNDERSTAND THE Church's teaching on prayer, we need to understand the purpose of our prayer life. The easiest explanation is that prayer is about getting us oriented toward Christ, putting us in a living and personal relationship, so that we are not just *near* but *focused on* God—within the presence of the Trinity. Praying in this way helps us to remember God in all moments of our lives.

Prayer is not simply the recitation of words on a page or thoughts in our heads. It is also physical—it includes the direction we face, our posture, our surroundings, what we touch and smell. It encompasses our whole being, because a human person is not simply a soul trapped in flesh. A human person is body, soul, and *nous*—that part of our being that is capable of apprehending God. One should not connect the nous with the intellect per se; rather the nous is understood as the eye of the soul. In order to fully appreciate this, we must step back for a moment and reflect on beginnings.

The Christian story begins with the notion that something has been lost. In our modern age of conveniences, it is easy to forget that, deep down, the Christian message is that we have lost our way—that we must *do something* to recover our truest nature, as our current state is lacking. The Christian life begins when we accept that we are out of step with what God originally intended. It is a journey of restoration, healing, and putting right what has been disfigured.

When I was younger, I used to think about Adam and Eve and the Fall as something that happened a really long time ago to characters I never knew. It was a narrative that told me about our origins and how we got into the mess we are in today.

But to begin the Christian life, one must start thinking of this story as one that is happening *right now*, to us. Adam and Eve are not just characters from a prehistoric past; they are you and me in our everyday lives.

Although it may seem odd, it is with Adam and Eve that we can begin to answer that simple yet profound question, How do I pray?

When we look at the human person, we must understand that we are not made of one thing. We are composed of the material and the immaterial. In that misshapen state initiated by Adam and Eve, the material became primary, and the immaterial took a back seat.

In this sense, the Fall is happening right now to you and me. We are almost entirely focused on the material, with our lives revolving around the wants and desires of our fallen nature, driven by the flesh. As St. Paul wrote, "I say then: Walk in the Spirit, and you shall not fulfill the lust of the flesh. For the flesh lusts against the Spirit, and the Spirit against the flesh; and these are contrary to one another, so that you do not do the things that you wish" (Gal. 5:16–17).

When my wife and I were dating, I acted like a gentleman—a man who was in love with a beautiful woman he hoped to marry. My desire for her translated into showering her with affection. But after we married and had spent some time together as husband and wife, I soon realized something profound: I was treating her terribly! My love for my wife was at odds with the way I treated her after we married, and it became quite clear that I was at odds with myself. I was doing exactly what St. Paul talks about in Romans: "For the good that I will *to do*, I do not do; but the evil I will not *to do*, that I practice" (Rom. 7:19). I wished to be married, and I loved my wife, but I was not acting in accordance with those feelings. I lacked the ability to love rightly.

We are often at odds with ourselves because of that misshapen state initiated by Adam and Eve. Our wants and desires are often directed at entirely the wrong things and are in need of reordering.

Prayer, then, must be about regaining and restoring the importance of the immaterial aspect of the human person, which has been ignored for so long. The flesh takes so much of our resources that we must recalibrate and give space to the immaterial. This is one of the foundations of our understanding of prayer's true purpose.

Prayer and Righteousness

In Scripture we see many uses of the term *righteous*. The Old Testament refers to God as righteous; Job is called a righteous man; and Jesus presents us with a model for righteousness throughout the Gospels. This is a very important term as we unfold the "how to" of prayer.

To be righteous is, in a sense, to be "right-ordered."

Saint Paul reminds us that, through Christ, we are to "put on the new man which was created according to God, in true righteousness and holiness" (Eph. 4:24), and that we are called to become "imitators of God" (Eph. 5:1). The Church understands this process as a restoration and a bringing to completion of that which was lost in the Fall.

One term for this restoration is *theosis*, which means becoming Christlike. Saint Paul wrote, "It is no longer I who live, but Christ who lives in me" (Gal. 2:20). In another place, he describes theosis this way: "For me to live is Christ" (Phil. 1:21). In prayer, we draw closer to Him—we get back on the path from which we fell—and begin this process of theosis by *right-ordering* ourselves through prayer.

Without this right-ordering prayer life, the material self takes over. If there is no engagement in prayer with our whole being, all our needs and desires tend to be dominated by the flesh, by the physical. The soul wrongly begins to serve the body instead of the other way around. That is the disorder in need of structure.

All of these considerations offer us a look at *why* we pray, which is of utmost importance as we move forward. But when many people ask how to pray, they are seeking the understanding of the actual *mechanics* of prayer and a prayer life. What should prayer look like, physically? How is it done? Where should one pray? What should one say, and when? We will now turn to these questions.

Prayer Involves Heart, Mind, and Body

THE ABOVE IS not to say, however, that prayer is a purely immaterial activity. Too often we begin by assuming that prayer should always be a mystical experience. We hope it will feel like being a conduit into the spiritual realm—if we say the right things, the heavens will open up to us, and a wave of euphoria will overtake us. For the mystics, this experience is possible and often happens.

But in reality, for many of us, prayer is more often like following a diet. A diet requires discipline and an understanding that what we put into our physical selves matters. We intuitively recognize that our consumption of a certain number and type of calories has a direct, causative connection to our overall health.

Many of us fail to see the relationship of the physical self to prayer, however, because it has become a mental exercise only. We neglect the physical self in favor of intellectual contemplation alone, resulting in a lack of understanding about what prayer truly is and, ultimately, in an incomplete picture of our relationship to God and what it means to be a human person, body and soul.

As with a food diet, everything matters. What we think in prayer and what we do with our physical selves on a daily basis affects our spiritual lives, so our prayer habits should reflect a desire to realign with God's purpose not only our minds, but our bodies as well.

How do we start?

Together and Alone, Alone and Together

WHEN I WAS a child, I quickly learned that Sunday morning was reserved for going to church. In fact, it was important to my parents that I, along with my siblings, received a perfect attendance certificate at the end of each church school year. However, I also experienced daily prayer at home. I remember spying on my grandfather, who prayed by himself each day in his bedroom. This influenced me greatly. I came to learn how important it was that I too pray, but privately, on my own, during time I set aside to commune with God. This I came to understand was part of the larger rhythm of going to church.

First we must understand that a proper prayer life includes personal and communal prayer times. Often when I meet with people about prayer, they have in mind that prayer is only done in private or that prayer only occurs on Sunday in church. Instead we teach that prayer is both. It is something we do alone:

"And when you pray, you shall not be like the hypocrites. For they love to pray standing in the synagogues and on the corners of the streets, that they may be seen by men. Assuredly, I say to you, they have their reward. But you, when you pray, go into your room, and when you have shut your door, pray to your Father who is in the secret place; and your Father who sees in secret will reward you openly." (Matt. 6:5–6)

It is also something we do together: "So He came to Nazareth, where He had been brought up. And as His custom was, He went into the synagogue on the Sabbath day" (Luke 4:16). In Holy Scripture we find many examples of both private and corporate prayer. They work together to refashion humanity.

Personal and communal prayer are linked and cannot be separated. If we ignore corporate or communal prayer, our personal prayers can become selfish and informed by our will alone, driven mostly by personal, individual desires that are often material in nature. Even the most reclusive hermits in Christian history were tied to the Body of Christ, the Church, through the communal prayers said together in the

21

Divine Services. Conversely, if we only pray when we go to church and never on our own, then attending the Divine Liturgy and other services becomes a dry experience. Services in church feel like an obligation to fulfill ancient rituals without meaning or power.

Saint Anthony the Great, after retreating to the desert as an ascetic monk, gained many followers. When one of them asked what he must do in order to please God, Abba Anthony responded, "Pay attention to what I tell you: whoever you may be, always have God before your eyes; whatever you do, do it according to the testimony of the holy Scriptures; in whatever place you live, do not easily leave it. Keep these three precepts, and you will be saved."[1] We most readily do these things by staying connected in our personal prayer to the communal prayer life of the Church.

A personal prayer rule is a freely imposed discipline. In it we commit to saying certain prayers at certain times. Such a rule is best developed with the help of another, often a spiritual father. No prayer rule should discount the prayers that are said by the faithful in the Divine Services, as they guide our personal prayer and ground us in humility by helping us understand first the needs and priorities set forth by

---

1   Benedicta Ward, trans., *The Desert Fathers: Sayings of the Early Christian Monks* (New York: Penguin Classics, 2003), 2.

the Church. The Church also aids us in knowing *what* to say in prayer and *how* to say it.

This means that what I pray in my home is largely informed and influenced by the Liturgy, but we should note that the Liturgy of Sunday is not the only communal prayer time of the Church. In a sense, Sunday's Divine Liturgy is the culmination of the entire rhythm of liturgical prayer, which involves hourly, daily, weekly, monthly, and seasonal prayers and divine services. If we do not experience this communal prayer, our personal prayer is lifeless and disconnected. Communal prayer has a unity—we not only *agree* on the prayer but we say the prayer together. These liturgical prayers are the common expression of the people of God. They are not simply an individualistic interpretation of feelings. As such, these prayers said together influence and find their way, literally, into what we say during our private time of prayer.

Christians regularly quote Matthew 18:20 (RSV), "For where two or three are gathered in my name, there am I in the midst of them," in relationship to corporate prayer and gathering. The word translated *gathered* comes from a Greek word that means "to lead together," understood as a "bringing together." When applied to prayer, a gathering is an assembly of the people of God in a common purpose. Think of a symphony, where many instruments come together. Corporate prayer is not just a group of individuals praying individually. It is human persons praying in communion (in agreement) with one another, as the Divine Liturgy states: "Let us love one another, that with one mind we may confess Father, Son, and Holy Spirit: Trinity, one in essence and undivided."

As noted earlier, the Epistle to the Hebrews refers to Christ as a minister and high priest. The Greek word *leitourgos* means to minister and serve the good of the people in an official capacity. It is also the root from which we derive the word *liturgy*. Liturgy means the common work of the people.

The Church has always seen the concepts of prayer and liturgy as inherently linked. If prayer is directed to the Divine Priest who serves liturgically in heaven, then it makes little sense to separate those concepts here on earth. The entire Epistle to the Hebrews, when read with this understanding in mind, shows clearly the relationship between liturgy and worship and that they ultimately cannot be differentiated without losing something.

In my Bible studies, I often point out that each of the Gospel accounts has specific, overarching themes. In the case of Matthew, the theme can be summarized with the simple phrase "listen and do." It is the Gospel that clearly lays out the basics of discipleship.

One could argue that Matthew comes first in order in the New Testament for this reason. We may take for granted the fact that the Bible is so readily accessible to us—our phones, computers, and other devices all provide instant access to any verse we want. As a result, many of us never question why the books are in a particular order. But the order is significant. The Church did not just throw the New Testament together chronologically or haphazardly. Matthew's Gospel helps us beginners through the "listen and do" theme of its message. It is helpful when building a life of prayer to notice that this theme is found in the beginning of the New Testament.

We can understand the importance of the Gospel of Matthew as the first book of the New Testament, because it needs to be read and understood first. And prominently featured in this book is a liturgical prayer, the Lord's Prayer, one given to us by no less than the Lord Himself!

All of this is to say that liturgical prayers, prayers connected to the Church and its practices, are exactly what the gospel writers have in mind when they speak of prayer. If we divorce prayer from this context, we end up lost in a sea of self-motivated words that are not connected to anything other than our own thoughts.

Yet there is still more to prayer beyond the

recitation of what the Church has prescribed. How we approach prayer *physically* matters a great deal, despite being discounted by much of modernity.

The Physical Mechanics of Prayer

CREATING A SPACE

So WHAT DOES prayer look like, and why?

One of the first things we can do is set apart a place for prayer—a place in our home where we go to pray. Think of prayer as the beginning of a journey and the building up of your faith as a pilgrimage: we get up from this place and go to another place. In Genesis 12:1, we read about the beginning of Abraham's journey (he was still called Abram at this point in his story). It begins with God calling him *out of the place he was* and *into the next place.* Like Abraham, we too must have a place where we *go* to pray in order to reenact that reality and tie us into the continuity of God's interaction with His people. In this way going to a place to pray is a pilgrimage like Abram's.

One of the biggest mistakes Christians make is to discount the idea that they need a place to pray. This attitude largely stems from the notion that prayer is just an intellectual pursuit—a mental or contemplative exercise. If prayer is only in your head, why do you need to be in a specific, physical space to pray?

Of course, prayer is not constrained by space or time, yet while we live in this world, place and time matter and even assist us.

We can view this idea of a place in many ways. The Israelites while wandering in the desert carried with them their place of prayer, the Tent of Meeting, setting it up whenever they arrived in a new encampment. This same idea is found in the familiar prayer, "Heavenly King, Comforter, the Spirit of Truth, present in all places and filling all things, Treasury of goodness and Giver of life: come and abide in us. Cleanse us from every stain of sin and save our souls, O Gracious Lord." This prayer to the Holy Spirit, which begins a set of prayers known as the Trisagion, suggests that while God is found everywhere, He can also be found in a place. Here that place is us, and the idea of setting up the place of meeting is found in the phrase "come and abide in us." The original Greek suggests the setting up of a tent inside of us, a place to meet God.

We should reiterate that our need to set up a specific, physical space to pray is conditioned by the belief that prayer does not have to be relegated to a singular place. Of course, one can pray anywhere and at all times—the Church has always affirmed this. But we as humans need sacred places set aside for certain purposes. This is yet another concept that we understand at a deeper level.

Consider the modern family as compared to generations past. Where did our ancestors eat dinner? In a dining room or, at the very least, around a common table. Family meals have been disappearing because we tend not to eat in a dedicated place anymore. We eat on couches, at countertops, and in cars. Dinner, for far too many, is no longer a special time. Eating is something we do because we have to so that we can get to the next thing. We have forgotten the importance of breaking bread together, *in communion* with one another.

We have abandoned the tradition of sitting down together for a meal in the name of convenience and distractions. If we eat in our cars, we can get to the next activity sooner; if we eat on the couch in front of the television, we do not have to worry about engaging in conversation. The sacred is replaced with the efficient.

Likewise, the utilitarian designs of some church buildings have taught us that a worship place does not matter. The warehouse-type layouts of some churches I see reflect a society that sees no more reverence in one place than the next. Any place is as good as any other, it seems.

When no place is more sacred than any other, the result is not that every place is elevated into being special; rather, every place is lowered to the mundane. Yet this approach ignores the origin story pointed out earlier. God created the entire universe and everything in it, but He placed Adam and Eve *in the Garden* as a special place. Even in the world's original state, some spaces were more sacred than others.

We should remember here the importance of the Incarnation. We understand as Christians that God has done something radical in becoming part of His creation—something beyond what is often discussed in modern Christian discourse. He has taken up matter itself and, in so doing, He has sanctified it; His nature—His very being—is intrinsically linked to material reality. By understanding this, we recognize that throughout Christ's ministry, matter itself became a vehicle for His grace. Through matter He communicated with creation, but, more importantly, He *healed* it.

Therefore we must not cast aside the physical for the spiritual only, as if they were somehow completely separate, with the spiritual being holy and the physical profane; that would be heretical thinking. Matter matters! So we must begin by setting up a physical space and making our pilgrimage to it in order to pray. That place is our prayer corner.

How DO WE set up this space? At a minimum, it should be well ordered, beautiful, and carefully tended. If a prayer corner is to be special, if it is to convey reverence, then it must be treated and maintained accordingly.

Keep a cross in your prayer corner. Although this may seem obvious, I see a growing number of churches that do not outwardly display this primary symbol of Christianity. So the importance of having a cross in your sacred space bears repeating.

Your prayer corner should include a candle or an oil lamp, both of which are preferable to electric lighting. Light produced by a flame creates an effect that is difficult to explain with words but is easily understood when used. (It is also important to note that if safety is a concern—such as when little children are present—it is okay to forgo an open flame.)

If you are comfortable with the use of icons in prayer (many who are exploring or new to the faith may not be), an icon of the Lord, one of the Virgin Mary (the Theotokos), and one of your patron saint (at minimum) should form the focal point of your prayer corner. Icons represent our understanding of both the physical nature of Christ and our present reality in the physical world, while also encouraging us to venerate those who have shown us how to live this life.

A prayer book is also very useful. There are numerous historical and liturgical prayers specific to different times of the day and year, special circumstances, and the church calendar, including the feast and fast days of the year. These are hard to commit to memory, even for a priest. A prayer book will focus your prayer life in alignment with the Church's liturgical calendar.

A Bible is important for numerous reasons, not the least of which is its position as foundational to our understanding of the life and teachings of Christ and the life of the Church. Holy Scripture forms the prayer life of the Church, so having and using it in your prayer corner should be fundamental. Reading Scripture is the same as prayer, because we *pray* the Scripture. The praying of Holy Scripture in our prayer time imitates what we find in communal prayer. Separating the Holy Writings from prayer for use in study alone diminishes their impact on our lives. One could say that the depths of Holy Scripture reveal themselves in the Church because she prays through and with the words of Scripture. This means that the Bible should never be understood or read only as an intellectual exercise, but first and foremost as prayer.

Your prayer corner can be adorned with a prayer cloth. Altars in the church are clothed as a place set apart. In an Orthodox temple, the holy table or altar stands away from the wall and is a focal point of the church; it is a sacred place and a meeting point between God and humanity. Similarly, your corner should be carefully clothed, indicating its separation from its surroundings. I recommend changing the cloth to reflect the seasons, thus keeping you aware of the relationship of the liturgical calendar to the physical world.

It is best if this space can face eastward, because Christ is the Risen Sun of the Church. By facing the east, we put behind us the place from which darkness comes. We see scriptural references to this concept. In the beginning of John's Gospel, we are told that in Christ "was life, and the life was the light of men. And the light shines in the darkness, and the darkness did not comprehend it" (John 1:4–5). In the physical world, the world that Christ entered, light begins in the east, so we face our churches and our prayer corners in the same direction in recognition of the True Light.

The tradition of facing east to pray dates to the earliest days of Christianity and is rooted in both Scripture and the Jewish custom of facing Jerusalem when praying. Matthew 24:27 tells us, "For as the lightning comes from the east and flashes to the west, so also will the coming of the Son of Man be."

The practice of facing east while praying was seen as a symbolic hope of Christ's second coming.[2] The Old Testament Book of Ezekiel contains multiple references to the tradition of facing east,[3] and several of the Church Fathers spoke of this practice. Saint John of Damascus tells us,

> It is not without reason or by chance that we worship towards the East. . . . Since, therefore, God is spiritual light, and Christ is called in the Scriptures Sun of Righteousness and Dayspring, the East is the direction that must be assigned to His worship. For everything good must be assigned to Him from Whom every good thing arises. Indeed the divine David also says, Sing unto God, ye kingdoms of the earth: O sing praises unto the Lord: to Him that rideth upon the Heavens of heavens towards the East. Moreover the Scripture also says, And God planted a garden eastward in Eden; and there He put the man whom He had formed: and when he had transgressed His command He expelled him and made him to dwell over against the delights of Paradise, which clearly is the West.[4]

If your prayer space can face east and also interplay with the natural environment, as in being next

---

2   See *The Orthodox Study Bible*'s note on Matthew 24:27.

3   E.g., Ezek. 43:4; 46:12.

4   John of Damascus, "Concerning Worship Towards the East," in *An Exact Exposition of the Orthodox Faith*, ed. Paul A. Boer, Sr., trans. S.D.F. Salmond, book IV, chapter 12.

to a window, for example, all the better. When we allow natural light to influence our prayer space, we are reminded of our lack of control. The rotation of the earth, the weather, and the seasons all remind us of the created world and its beauty. Connecting nature to your prayer space can have a profound effect, because creation itself is God's work. Matter matters! The physical world is not to be discounted and cast away in favor of the spiritual. We must still be in awe of His creation and our place within it. A window and natural light remind us that we do not control the light. We are not the source of the light; God is.

Your prayer space can be on a table or a shelf, and it can be small—it doesn't need to take up much space. You do not need a shrine taking up half of your room.

Multiple prayer spaces in a home are also ideal. Having a personal space for each family member plus one for the whole family and guests helps remind us that both the Church and our prayer life are hierarchical and communal. Setting up one's home with several prayer spaces, if possible, grounds us in this reality.[5] God set man as a steward over creation to

---

5   See *Blueprints for the Little Church: Creating an Orthodox Home* by Elissa Bjeletich and Caleb Shoemaker (Chesterton, IN: Ancient Faith Publishing, 2016) and *Making God Real in*

claim it, beautify it, and sanctify it. Stories like St. Seraphim's feeding of the bear show us a way to see the importance of sanctifying our surroundings, not simply in a utilitarian sense, but in the context of *holiness*. Creating spaces for prayer in the kitchen, in the laundry area, at the office, and elsewhere is helpful to remind us in every place we go of the need to commune with God through prayer. It is interesting that the Church views the home as an extension of itself: it is the "little church." This connection reminds us that the little church follows and is connected to the rhythms of the big church, and vice versa.

On a personal note, in my own prayer corner I have noticed a significant difference after I began using an oil lamp as a source of light. The ancient tradition of lighting a lamp is hard to miss in Scripture, as it is given a great deal of attention. In Jesus' parable of the bridegroom in Matthew 25, for example, "those who were ready" were those who *carefully tended* their lamps; those who did not do so missed the bridegroom, and the door was shut to them. (Of course you should only leave an unattended oil lamp lit if it is safe to do so.)

The careful, physical tending of my prayer space reminds me that I need to be vigilant. Maintaining

the Orthodox Christian Home by Anthony Coniaris (Minneapolis, MN: Light & Life Publishing Co., 1977).

a light through filling a lamp and trimming its wick is a hands-on approach to prayer that ties the material and immaterial by prompting me to be watchful.

The oil lamp also grounds me to something timeless. Modernity has largely divorced us from the importance of caring for something over the long term. We live in an era when everything can be replaced almost instantly. I can order a brand-new version of something I broke and have it shipped to my home in one or two days. If we are not careful, this convenience can become ingrained in how we view life as a whole—everything is cheap, disposable, and readily available.

Tending to an oil lamp ties me to ancient, timeless practices while keeping me vigilant and mindful of the present time. Just as a gardener cannot plant something once and sit back, assuming all the work is done, I do not set up my prayer corner once and call it done. I keep an oil lamp as a reminder to be ever present and heedful in my prayer life.

POSTURE

PERHAPS YOU ARE used to praying immediately upon rising from bed or directly before going to sleep. There is nothing wrong with this, and in fact I encourage it. I would, however, caution you to prepare yourself to enter your sacred prayer space.

It is good to go to our prayer corner "robed" or dressed rather than in our underwear. This habit is another way of separating the space as being sacred and different from the rest of our house while also putting ourselves in the right-ordered frame of mind. Tending to our physical selves influences our prayer life.

In Scripture, the old man is cast off, and the new man is put on. Saint Paul tells us, "Do not lie to one another, since you have put off the old man with his deeds, and have put on the new *man* who is renewed in knowledge according to the image of Him who created him" (Col. 3:9–10). We can symbolize this truth with our clothing during prayer. Coming to our prayer corner disheveled and sloppy is certainly not forbidden or innately sinful, but is it ideal? Many social scientists have demonstrated that how we dress does, in fact, influence how we view the world around us.[6]

In the Gospel of Matthew, Christ tells the parable of the wedding feast, in which a guest arrives without a wedding garment and subsequently is thrown out (Matt. 22:11–13). Given that the host

6   M. L. Slepian, S. N. Ferber, J. M. Gold, and A. M. Rutchick, "The Cognitive Consequences of Formal Clothing," *Social Psychological and Personality Science* 6, no. 6 (2015), https://doi.org/10.1177/1948550615579462.

would have provided all the guests with proper garments, this particular guest's lack of compliance is really a refusal of an offered gift—a rejection of that which God has freely offered. We robe ourselves in order to remind ourselves of the gifts of grace and baptism. As St. Paul states in the Epistle to the Galatians, "For as many of you as were baptized into Christ have put on Christ" (Gal. 3:27). The allusion to robing is unmistakable.

Of course, this practice varies based on individual needs. We cannot, for example, assume that everyone should go to their prayer corner wearing the nicest business suit or dress on the market. There is great latitude in the Church's teachings on appropriate attire, but what is important to understand is that the way we *approach* the altar—be it in a sanctuary or in our home—matters.

We do not go to church and sit on a recliner with a cup of tea and a blanket across our laps. We are not jumping around, being loud, and making the service an emotionally charged event, either. Our physical posture before the Lord should be standing or kneeling. It should be *reverent*. This helps us to focus the mind and the heart on God. We learn through our posture to stand reverently and thus prayerfully before God.

We can stand upright with hands lifted, we can

stand on our knees, or we can be prostrate—on our knees with forehead to the ground. These are the three primary positions of prayer, which we will discuss in just a moment. Of course, if these postures are not physically possible for some of us, this does not mean that we cannot pray. God would never reject our prayer because of our physical position, but what we are pointing out is that some postures assist our prayer more than others.

It is important to remember here that our posture includes more than just how we stand. It involves the way we *approach* God and behave in the physical space of prayer. Our approach directs our spirits to a certain way of living and acting. Look at places like a frat house or a sports bar. Abundant visual and physical cues in these places gear the mind toward certain ways of thinking. Grocery stores are laid out in specific ways to help drive customers toward certain items, because marketers understand something that much of Christianity has lost—that we need physical aids to guide us, both in time and place.

A physical space and posture that are sober, set apart, and reverent are of great benefit to any and all Christians, as they help align us with God and His Church. In order to embrace these practices fully, however, we need to establish a routine. Although the idea of routine comes across to many modern Christians as chore-like, the simple fact is that we cannot rely on praying only when we *feel* like doing so.

There is much benefit to be gained from routine, which we will now examine.

Have a keepable rule of prayer that you do by discipline.

—*Fr. Thomas Hopko,*
"55 Maxims of the Christian Life"

ESTABLISHING A ROUTINE for prayer is certainly not a bad thing. Remember that when the apostles asked the Lord how to pray, He did not say, "Pray what is on your heart at the moment." He gave them a *liturgical* prayer.

In the Book of Acts, as we shared earlier, the early Church "continued steadfastly in the apostles' doctrine and fellowship, in the breaking of bread, and in prayers" (Acts 2:42). As *The Orthodox Study Bible* reminds us, however, *"Prayers* is literally *'the* prayers' in Greek (*tais proseuchais*), referring to specific liturgical prayers."[7] Liturgical prayers, specifically the Psalms, were a normal part of Jewish life and had been for centuries.

These prayers were also conducted at certain

---

7   See *The Orthodox Study Bible's* note on Acts 2:42.

times of the day. Acts 3:1 tells us that "Peter and John went up together to the temple at the hour of prayer, the ninth *hour*." Observance of the hours of prayer—6 AM, 9 AM, 12 PM (noon), and 3 PM—had been a Jewish custom for centuries, as evidenced in the Books of Psalms and Daniel. The early Church adopted this custom from its beginning, as we can see in the Book of Acts.

To forgo routine and liturgical prayers, then, is to ignore exactly what Scripture is teaching us. Liturgical prayers were quite literally the practice of the very people who wrote the New Testament. So how do we do this in our own home?

It is best to start with a routine we can keep and to add to this slowly and steadily over time. Many begin with reciting their prayers in the evening, before dinner or bedtime, while others begin with saying them in the morning before starting their day. What is important is that we begin and establish a habit of daily prayer. In time we should pray at various times—morning, midday, evening, and so on. In time we also learn the value of praying as we begin our work for the day, when we encounter something hard or unexpected, at mealtimes, and continuously with every breath we take. This last form of prayer is typically practiced by learning and reciting the Jesus Prayer: "Lord Jesus Christ, Son of God, have mercy on me, a sinner." Below we will say a bit more about what to actually say when praying.

WE CAN APPROACH our prayer corner by first making a prostration. This is referred to as a *metanoia* (pronounced *meh-TAHN-yuh*), of which there are two types, small and great. The small metanoia involves bending at the waist and touching one's right hand to the ground, then standing upright while making the sign of the cross. A great metanoia involves getting down on one's knees, putting one's forehead all the way to the floor, then standing upright while making the sign of the cross.

These actions have symbolic significance. The word *metanoia* also denotes repentance. In the parable of the prodigal son, the lost son recognized his fallen state and his sin against his father while he was among the swine. "I will arise and go to my father, and will say to him, 'Father, I have sinned against heaven and before you, and I am no longer worthy to be called your son. Make me like one of your hired servants'" (Luke 15:18–19). In a sense, the story of the prodigal begins with his falling and then arising.

We know that we were created upright, able to stand before God in the Garden. In life, as in the Fall, we experience something else. We fall short, and we do things that bring us to a low estate, lowering us from our place of honor and glory as icons of God. However, we were not created to live this way. In the parable of the prodigal son we are reminded of this central narrative of our fall and our return.

Midway into the story we find the prodigal on all fours, like an animal. He has lost his way, his humanity, and his ability to stand aright. Through his loose living and squandering of his inheritance, he has entered a fallen state. He has abandoned his relationship with his loving father and has become attached to the material world. He has lost himself. In this condition one might easily believe that a return to our right standing before God can come about through taking something from the material world—*If I do X, Y, or Z, then that will solve my problems*, we say to ourselves. We search for solutions to problems with material efforts. In the parable we read, "And he would gladly have filled his stomach with the pods that the swine ate, and no one gave him *anything*" (15:16).

As we said earlier, it is important to notice what happens next in the story, for in a sense this is where the story truly begins. The prodigal says, "I will arise and go to my father."

In the physical movement of making a prostration, I lower myself, as did the prodigal, to eat what the swine are eating. I have wrongly become connected to the earth and earthly minded. But the good news is that, through Christ and His Cross, I rise up and can once again stand upright before God. We demonstrate this by standing up while making the sign of the cross in reverence for the One who brings us up from the swine.

As I stand before God, however, I have learned that it is likely I am not going to remain standing forever. So I prostrate myself another time, recognizing that I come before Him and fall once again, but now in humility before my Creator. A prostration is the process of putting the body in its proper place—below the soul. We prostrate ourselves in humility and place the whole self—body, mind, and spirit—before God.

This can be done three or thirty times. The exact number matters less than the action, but some say the typical order is two or three prostrations, then veneration of our icons, then a third or fourth prostration. This is the traditional approach, but it can be adjusted. It is important to go over the details of this and other prayer practices with your spiritual father.

When we venerate an icon, we kiss the hem of Christ's or the saint's garment, the hand, or the foot. This is yet another sign of humility. Venerating icons is, for many new Orthodox Christians, a somewhat awkward practice. For now, it is important simply to understand that the veneration of icons is a deeply rich tradition that pours directly out from a proper theological understanding. We are *physical* beings who follow after other physical beings who showed us how life can be led in the physical Church. Icons are another reminder that tie us to that physical reality.

Now that we have lit our candle or lamp, made our prostrations, and venerated the icons, what do we say?

Our Prayer Rule

BEGIN BY GATHERING your thoughts and warming your heart toward God. Standing reverently in your place of prayer, as best as you can, turn your whole self toward God. In such a state we attempt to pray our prayers without distraction.

You should consult your spiritual father about exactly when to pray and which prayers to say. At the minimum I encourage people to start in the morning by thanking God for the gift of a new day and praising Him for His many blessings. The morning is also a good time to ask for God's wisdom for what we will encounter and to pray and reflect over the daily scripture reading and the feast or season we are celebrating within the liturgical calendar. In the evening it is helpful to thank God for the day that has passed, reflect on our day, and repent of any sins we have committed. Additionally, it is important in the evening to remember in prayer those people and situations we experienced and for which we need God's help. In addition, there are many different prayers for different times of the day, different days of the liturgical calendar, and for special occasions and circumstances. This is where our prayer book comes in handy.

Do not shy away from reading prayers out of a book. Doing so in no way takes away from the reverence of a proper prayer life, and in fact adds to it by showing us how the saints of the Church have prayed for centuries and by preventing our minds from wandering. Within our prayer time we can, of course, reserve time for stillness and for prayers that come from the heart. Being silent and still helps us learn to quiet our minds and hearts. This in turn helps us guard our thoughts, hearts, and actions. Within this framework of prayer as given by Christ and His Church, we are kept from straying too far.

Many saints and elders of the Church have given advice on what exactly to say and use from the Church's treasure trove of prayers. It is important to learn and heed their advice by adjusting their teachings to your life through speaking with your priest. If you are unable to do so, simply read from your prayer book the prayers assigned for the particular time of day. It is helpful to memorize as many of the prayers as you can, as memorization can aid us in saying our prayers, helping them to become embedded in our hearts.

We also learn much from our time in the divine services. In them we learn the order of prayer, its rhythms, and the many ways the Church prays. The Church introduces us to the various traditions and resources of prayer, and these are easily transmitted into our private prayer time. Remember that our private prayer is connected, informed, and enriched by our communal prayer. Praying on our own is also important to the prayer life of the community. We know that private prayer greatly edifies the Church, and the relationship between the two is essential. Without both, much is lost.

It is worth making a special note here: Many ask whether or not it is acceptable to use a smartphone or some other digital device that can access several Bible versions and prayer books, in place of a physical book, for our prayer routine. Are they equivalent, or are there inherent problems with electronic devices that should prevent us from adopting them into our prayer corners?

The Church does not have a problem with or fear of new technology. Individual books were, at one time, very new technology, after all! The primary concern, however, relates to distraction.[8] Does your electronic device have alerts and notifications that draw your attention and will distract you during your prayers? Will the various features of your technology divert your focus away from where it should be?

Just as a honeybee can extract nectar from a poisonous plant, we can draw out that which is good from a source that may contain toxic elements, so long as we are aware of its potential pitfalls. Along these lines, it is vital to understand one's own weaknesses. Some people may be more capable than others of turning off distractions or using certain technologies for good rather than bad. In this area we once again see the importance of a priest or spiritual father who can help us navigate these decisions, lest we make them using only our own will.

It is also important to grasp where we are in our journey with the aid of a priest or spiritual father, in order that we do not overcommit or become self-directed in our efforts. Many who are new to the Orthodox Faith begin by assuming they can follow the same prayer rules as those in a monastery, only to burn out quickly when they realize the difficulties of doing so. Work with a spiritual father, and be patient!

---

8   See *Reclaiming Conversation: The Power of Talk in a Digital Age* by Sherry Turkle (New York: Penguin Press, 2015).

To finish our prayers, we simply do a metanoia in the same order as when we began. If it is safe to do so, we leave the lamp burning.

Summary

I SPEAK WITH many converts and inquirers who have been brought up to believe that every prayer must be spontaneous; somehow praying "in the spirit" means that prayer must be made up on the spot according to whatever they are *feeling* at that given moment. But remember, when the disciples asked the Lord how to pray, *He gave them a prayer.* So starting with the Our Father as a standard rule of prayer is exactly in line with what the Church has taught for two thousand years.

Praying liturgical prayers keeps us grounded in the prayer of the Body of Christ, even as we make our own pilgrimage. When we reject these prayers, which have been handed down to us by the Church and its saints over the centuries, our prayers can become individualistic, self-motivated, and self-serving—the opposite of what worship is supposed to be.

Learn from the Church. Learn from the saints. They have great wisdom that will at once humble you and lift you up, helping you recognize the Way which has been lost and pointing you back toward righteousness.

Our Father, who art in heaven, hallowed be Thy name. Thy kingdom come, Thy will be done, on earth as it is in heaven. Give us this day our daily bread, and forgive us our trespasses as we forgive those who trespass against us. And lead us not into temptation but deliver us from evil.

CHAPTER TWO

Almsgiving

"When you do a charitable deed ..."
(Matthew 6:3)

W HEN MY DAUGHTER was young, she was play-
ing on the bed and fell awkwardly. Her neck
twisted in a grotesque fashion, and I felt it throughout my whole body. Her pain was my pain, her suffering was my suffering, her flesh was my flesh. Her
hurt was immediate, and I thought nothing of myself.

Every parent can relate to this. In those moments
when our children do something harmful to themselves, their pain is not something you just notice—it
is *your* pain as well.

In most of us, however, this empathetic ability rarely extends past our own family members.
Although we are quick to take on the suffering of our
immediate family as our own, doing so for complete

strangers is a challenge; yet it is one we must be willing to face, as the spiritual discipline of almsgiving is essential to our journey.

In Matthew's recounting of Jesus' Sermon on the Mount, the opening words of chapter 6 are focused on the spiritual practice of almsgiving. Many versions of the Bible translate the key words—*dikaiosune*, meaning "righteousness," in verse 1, and *eleemosune*, meaning "mercifulness," in verses 2 and 3—as "righteousness," "alms," and "charity," or good/charitable deeds. In English, unfortunately, the translation and the meaning we ascribe to these two words are rather flat.

From the first word, *dikaiosune*, which comes from *dikaois*, "righteous," we should get the sense of living with integrity and virtue, of thinking and acting in a correct way. With *eleemosune*, from *eleos*, "mercy," we get the sense of showing mercy toward those in need. The act of love toward the other seeks to restore both the recipient and the giver.

To be righteous and merciful means you can't live in this world without heartfelt concern for others. In such a state, acts of love are not limited to offering money or material support, nor is the act transactional in nature. There is no sense of superiority or pride. Instead, the act of love is shared and healing. With this in mind we use the words *alms*, *almsgiving*, or *charity*.

Almsgiving and the Kingdom of God

THE PARABLE OF the good Samaritan is an often-used example of being charitable to those in need, but it is rarely discussed as an illustration of our place in the Kingdom of God. Christ shared the story as a way of saying that if our religious pursuits do not lead us to help those around us, then we have fallen short.

In Luke 10 Jesus tells the story of a man who had been beaten, robbed, and left for dead, "but a certain Samaritan, as he journeyed, came where he was. And when he saw him, he had compassion" (v. 33). Our modern use of the word *compassion* leads us to believe that it is a thought—an attitude toward another person or persons. Even Merriam-Webster's dictionary reflects this understanding by using the words "sympathetic consciousness" in its definition. But the original Greek, *splagchnizomai*, has a much more *physical* component. A more literal translation would be, "he felt in his guts the pain of his brother and fellow man." Like the pain I felt in my gut when my daughter twisted her neck, the Samaritan's compassion was not just a thought or a general attitude but a physical pain. He could not distinguish between the pain he felt and the suffering of the man left for dead.

Given that the Samaritan is an image of Christ coming down from heaven, this parable introduces us to a stark reality, namely, that Christ on the Cross felt *our* pain and not just His own. He physically held compassion (*splagchnizomai*) in His guts.

This meaning leads us directly to the conclusion that we are not rightly ordered, as discussed in the previous section, regarding charity and compassion, and we desperately need to be. Compassion is crucial to our place in His Kingdom.

In Matthew 25, Jesus shares the parable of the Last Judgment, in which He explains that those who are blessed to inherit the Kingdom will be placed at the right hand of God. He explains that when He was hungry, they gave Him food; when He was thirsty, they gave Him drink; when He was a stranger, they took Him in; when He was naked, they clothed Him; when He was sick, they visited Him; and when He was in prison, they went to Him (vv. 35–36). "Assuredly I say to you, inasmuch as you did *it* to one of the least of these My brethren, you did *it* to Me" (v. 40).

I find it interesting to note that when those who have been declared righteous hear that they have been compassionate toward others, their reply is, "Lord, when did we see You hungry and feed *You*, or thirsty, and give *You* drink? When did we see You a stranger and take *You* in, or naked and clothe *You*? Or when did we see You sick, or in prison, and come to You?" (vv. 37–39). It seems that they are not aware of their love; rather, it is a part of them. The Lord is not commending them for their calculated effort to get involved in charitable giving; they would recognize and remember such sacrificial work. So it must be that these actions had become normal to them. It may help to consider that love is a state of being first and that the act of love comes next, being rooted in our transformation. This is the basis for *agape*, sacrificial love.

He follows this with a strong contrast to those who did not feed, clothe, or visit the least of His brethren, stating, "'Assuredly, I say to you, inasmuch as you did not do *it* to one of the least of these, you did not do *it* to Me.' And these will go away into everlasting punishment, but the righteous into eternal life" (Matt. 25:45–46).

The message here is clear: the criterion of judgment is sacrificial love.

This is a difficult pill to swallow, even for most Christians. Can any of us say that we have, at every possible turn, fed, clothed, and ministered to the least of His brethren? Are any of us truly able to look in the mirror with confidence that we have been as charitable as possible?

If you are like me, you have a need to become more loving and compassionate. But many do not seek to develop these virtues, nor are they aware of the essential role they play in the restoration of the image of God in us. Once we do see their importance, we can ask ourselves, How do we go about rightly ordering ourselves toward a life of alms?

Thanks be to God, the Church has the answer to this. Much like our prayer life, however, the remedy requires discipline.

Face to Face

BEING DISCIPLINED ABOUT charity is important. From the littlest to the grandest action, we must let go of the notion that charity only happens when we *feel* compelled to act, as if the desire to be compassionate will simply materialize out of thin air.

In truth, almsgiving is much simpler than that, even if it requires more effort on our part.

The first step is to understand that we are conditioning ourselves either toward compassionate almsgiving or away from it. We create environments in which giving alms is either part of our reality or it is not.

As a way of thinking about this, consider your home as a metaphor for your life. Is your house filled with so many material goods that there is no longer any room for other people? Now imagine that a friend needs a place to sleep for a few nights, but your spare bedroom is packed full as storage and therefore unusable. In order to allow your friend to stay, you need to *create a physical space* in your home.

Our spiritual lives are similar in that we need to create space—actual, physical space—that conditions us toward compassionate almsgiving rather than away from it. As Christians, we must have physical encounters with those in need. Online donations are great, but the physical interaction is fundamental to this process. Taking small steps toward creating those opportunities is the foundation of this discipline.

When I was first attempting to grow in charity, I spoke with my parish priest. I was fairly certain I didn't have much to offer. He gave me profound advice by suggesting, "Just start to give something, no matter how small, of your time, your talents, and your treasure. If you do so, God will bless you, and He will increase your efforts slowly but surely."

The key element is the encounter, the face-to-face interaction, with our brothers and sisters. If we look at the icon of the parable of the good Samaritan, we see the priest and the Levite looking *away* from the suffering man as they walk by him. In contrast, Christ, who symbolizes the good Samaritan, is shown touching and looking *into and at* the suffering man. He is not afraid to touch, look into the eyes, and hold the hand of the one who is in need.

Having a physical interaction with someone in need means you cannot walk by or stay in the shadows. Anyone who has had an actual conversation with an orphan can tell you that the experience goes far beyond simply putting a check in the mail or donating online, both for the child and for the giver.

When we are in touch with those in need, not only do we have an opportunity to express care, but proximity with those in need works on *us* in a spiritual way that is difficult to define, despite being easily noticeable. As Orthodox Christians, we know that change occurs in relationship, in contrast with the arm's-length mentality of writing a check, serving on the board of a charity without being personally involved, or being a member of a church that simply *talks* about charitable giving.

Christianity in many ways has become depersonalized because, in the emphasis on the individual, we have lost sight of the relational. In our societal efforts to prize the individual and offer physical cushions between ourselves and those less fortunate, we neglect to create the space that allows for connectedness to those in need. The hyperindividualism of modern society enables us to live day to day without ever encountering the poor or needy. This distancing has resulted in a psychological and spiritual poverty, because it betrays the truth that one must exist within community with others to understand the personal.

Individualism has also affected the relationships closest to us. Being charitable even to our family and closest friends has become increasingly difficult. Our love even for them may grow cold as we become increasingly self-directed and self-centered. Getting what I want when I want it all the time eliminates charity, even in the home.

So how do we start taking those steps in the right direction? I suggest starting simply and building from there. It may help to consider that we are not asked to do great things, but rather, as Mother Teresa said, to do small things with great love.

Talents and Passions

I THINK IT is helpful to pray and think about what we can do as an offering of love to others. Often this is something connected with things we do well, love, or enjoy. For example, a person with a talent like book-keeping can volunteer in a practice that serves the poor—doing accounting work for a small charity, or even preparing tax returns for a family in need who struggles with doing that type of thing. Or, if we like horseback riding, we may find a center that offers therapeutic riding to people with disabilities. Maybe we love to garden, so planting flowers and trees for those who do not have them—remember, matter matters!—is a valuable offering.

The possibilities are as varied and numerous as the talents among us. Take something you already love—teaching, for example—and find a way to leverage that. Is there a program already in existence for helping those in need by using your talents? Are there people in your community who cannot afford an education but are in need of educational development that an adept teacher could provide?

Perhaps you are skilled in trades such as plumbing or construction; these are always in great need by those who cannot afford them as professional services. We are quick to think of "feeding the poor" in relation to charity, but we often neglect to include basic heating and indoor plumbing within that same context.

In modern Christianity, we have attempted to homogenize people in terms of what they give and what their own gifts are. Soup kitchens and prison ministries seem to be held as the ideals for charitable offerings, while we discount the importance of other ventures. But we are not all Saint Basil the Great. Not everyone possesses the skills to minister in prisons or help special-needs children, so forcing narrow ideas of service causes innumerable problems.

Monasteries provide us with an example of suiting a person's service to his gifts. Given the lack of connection we have to these havens of prayer in Christianity today, it is not surprising that most people do not understand how they operate. Non-monastics are often surprised to discover that new monks are not simply placed wherever needs dictate, but rather according to their own abilities. The monk who is gifted at gardening is placed in the gardens; those gifted in singing are placed in the choir. Monasteries understand that the talents of each person come from God, and they are used accordingly. It would be a waste, after all, to take a young monk with a beautiful voice and tell him he could only wash dishes and not sing!

In the parable of judgment mentioned above, Christ praises those who fed Him, took Him in, clothed Him, and visited Him while He was sick or in prison, not realizing that it was Christ they were helping. Unfortunately, many modern Christians see this parable as a closed model; they view Christ's examples as being the *only* ways of helping those in need. But this is not the centuries-old understanding of His Church.

Feeding and clothing the poor and visiting the

sick and imprisoned should always remain vitally important, and we should never turn our backs on an opportunity to help in those areas. But the Church does not view these as the only available methods of almsgiving. Saint Gregory of Nyssa (fourth century), for example, was known for his incredible intellect and devoted it to the growth of Orthodoxy. Saint Marcian (fifth century) used his substantial inheritance on the building and beautifying of churches.

A personal favorite story of mine is that of St. Nektarios of Aegina (nineteenth and twentieth centuries), who was a principal at a high school. After finding out that the janitor of the school was about to be fired because of poor performance, St. Nektarios quietly accomplished all of the janitor's work, thus leading everyone to believe the man was doing a better job. Recognizing this act of charity, the janitor, who had a family and desperately needed the money his job provided, began to turn his life around and work harder. The fact that St. Nektarios did this for him without expecting any credit inspired a huge change in the man's life. Almsgiving can be taking responsibility for the failures around us and making a change.

One way of understanding this idea is to consider our lives and their many stages. We are all, at various times in our lives, capable of different things. It makes perfect sense that we would not expect a child to visit those in prison, nor would we presume they should be housing and caring for wayward strangers. A young child cannot even leave the home on her own, but she can certainly be taught to be charitable to her siblings in her own home. So it is for those in other stages of life—the plan for almsgiving must be modified to what is appropriate for our current circumstances.

But there is no reason we cannot apply this same type of thinking to everyone. If a single, working mother comes to me feeling guilty about not spending time in a soup kitchen, do I admonish her and tell her that she needs to be more active in feeding the poor? No, I suggest almsgiving *in her home*. How can she be more charitable toward her children with the gifts and abilities she has?

The Lord has not taught us to give alms in a certain way; He gives us options based on where we are and what we have. Often when people read the story of the rich man who asked Christ what he must do be saved, they see His direction of "sell whatever you have and give to the poor" (Mark 10:21) as being an order for all people at all times, and they realize how daunting that would be. But they neglect a crucial aspect of the passage and thus fail to recognize the intent within. As the beginning of the verse states, "Then

Jesus, looking at him, *loved him*" (emphasis mine). This indicates that Christ was speaking *to this man*, having understood what *he* was attached to; "loved him" indicates a knowledge and understanding of the person that goes beyond a simple, blanket rule.

It would be unfair to state that this teaching should be applied equally to all people. It may be beneficial to understand that it was, for that man, the key to unlocking his heart. The key here is that one person's weakness may not be the same as another's and, in fact, that our differences can be used to benefit the whole body.

As St. Paul wrote, "And He Himself gave some *to be* apostles, some prophets, some evangelists, and some pastors and teachers," that "from whom the whole body, joined and knit together by what every joint supplies, according to the effective working by which every part does its share, causes growth of the body for the edifying of itself in love" (Eph. 4:11, 16). The reality is that we are, as a whole, *better* for embracing the differences of individuals as they bring their unique talents to the Church.

The book *In the Heart of the Desert: The Spirituality of the Desert Fathers and Mothers* records many sayings of Syncletica of Alexandria (fourth century). Addressing the ill, she once said, "Truly, fasting and sleeping on the ground are set before us on account of our sensuality. However, if illness weakens this sensuality, then the reason for these practices is superfluous. For this is the great asceticism: to control oneself in illness and to sing hymns of thanksgiving to God."[9] In accordance with this idea, the Church understands that our charity exists *within our lives*. Rather than demanding we become someone we are not and try to do the impossible, the Church walks with us where we are and fully appreciates our current reality, encouraging acts of charity and kindness completely within the context of our present situation.

We would do well to remember here the words of St. Paul in his letter to the Corinthians: "Let each one remain in the same calling in which he was called" (1 Cor. 7:20). While the call to follow Christ is certainly a radical one, He is not asking businessmen, teachers, or doctors to be something they are not!

If almsgiving were a bus, then we would all need to be on it, but we would not all need to be in the front seat. We need all the seats occupied in order to distribute the vast needs of human persons to all involved, and in order to do that, we need to encourage every individual to use his own talents.

---

9   John Chryssavgis, *In the Heart of the Desert: The Spirituality of the Desert Fathers and Mothers* (Bloomington, IN: World Wisdom, Inc.), 30.

All of this begins with the discipline of taking those initial, small steps in the direction of having a charitable heart for our neighbor. As stated in my earlier example, the goal should be to start small and *stick with it*. If all you can do is drop a dime in the poor box or give five minutes of your time every week to a charitable effort, then start there. Do not set yourself up for failure by imagining what "perfect love" looks like and immediately trying to do all of it or failing to initiate a first step because it seems impossible.

What often stops us from giving is the idealization of the imagined goal. We have a fantasy of what alms-giving is supposed to look like, and we are intimidated by it. But this is the devil's trickery. The idea that we must do things perfectly and are inadequate if we do not will lead to serious self-doubt and fatalistic beliefs about our spiritual progress. Be aware that this is exactly where the evil one wants us—believing that we might as well give up.

We can only do so much. Start small, stick to it, and God will build on that. As a parish priest, I have seen this happen countless times. I instruct people to start at a level that they know they can consistently accomplish and not to give up on that small step. Every time they do this, the transformation is amazing and clearly noticeable. Before long, both their efforts and capacity for giving are transformed into something greater than they previously thought possible.

Toxic Charity

MUCH HAS BEEN written recently on the concept of toxic charity—the idea that, in some cases, charity actually *hurts* those it is intended to help. The numerous reasons for this problem fall beyond the scope of this book, but what is important to cover here is how it relates to the subject of almsgiving for individuals at a parish level.

People regularly ask me how to differentiate between a positive charitable effort and one that may cause more harm than good. They want their efforts to have a positive effect and are leery of scams—rightly so, in this day and age, unfortunately.

How I answer this question, however, depends a great deal on the person, and this is yet another reason why having a spiritual father is so important. Does the person give freely of his possessions and wealth to anyone and everyone who asks, possibly to the detriment of his own family (and even of those to whom he is giving)? Then he lacks discernment. I would advise him to better understand the possible downsides of this habit in a practical sense: "Behold,

I send you out as sheep in the midst of wolves. Therefore be wise as serpents and harmless as doves" (Matt. 10:16).

Or does the person find any and every possible excuse *not* to give, talking herself out of charity through a constant overanalysis of every possible downside of giving? Then I would suggest she let go of the control she desperately desires, as her wealth has a hold on her at a deep level.

Many people fit into these categories (and many others fall somewhere in between), so offering a singular answer is difficult. With all of these considerations, we must not overlook the necessity of *physical connection* with those in need. We cannot separate ourselves from poverty, regardless of our personal disposition. Recall that in the parable of the good Samaritan, the Samaritan did not pass the beaten man by and hire someone else to take care of him. He stopped and physically connected with him, attending to his needs in a deep and personal way.

In other words, regardless of our talents and personalities, we are called to interact tangibly with those in need. Remember, matter matters!

CHAPTER THREE

Fasting

"Moreover, when you fast ..." (Matthew 6:16)

W HAT IS THE first commandment in the Garden of Eden? It is *not* to eat something—a command to fast (Gen. 2:17).

What did Christ do immediately following His Baptism? The synoptic Gospels (Matthew, Mark, and Luke) all record Him being led into the wilderness, where He fasted for forty days. After this time of turning to God through fasting and prayer, Christ is tempted by the devil.

I start here because in our modern world, the idea of fasting seems archaic and even self-abusing. The concept conjures images from the Middle Ages such as self-flagellation or some type of penance. We convince ourselves that fasting was an ancient, letter-of-the-law practice that should be associated more with pharisaical living than being a "spiritual" Christian.

Yet should we be so quick to dismiss something that was part of God's first command to man and also the first action Christ took after His Baptism? There is an ordered, healthy manner of existence in which humanity comes to be in rhythm with God's design, and the Church has taught for thousands of years that fasting is an integral part of that rhythm.

We know, for example, that forgiveness is healthy for the mind and body. A significant body of research points to both the physical and psychological benefits of forgiveness, including a reduction in heart disease and anxiety disorders.[10] This comes as no surprise to the Church, as we know that the author of human existence is God.

We should therefore be careful not to dismiss a practice as being old or irrelevant simply because our culture has done so. The first thing humanity was asked to do was fast, and the first thing Christ did after baptism was fast. In light of this, it seems we should take fasting quite seriously.

---

10   Kristen Weir, "Forgiveness Can Improve Mental and Physical Health," *American Psychological Association* 48, no. 1 (January 2017).

Why Do We Fast?

THE FAST AFFECTS the human body, and what we do in the body affects the soul. A human being is an integrated reality, as previously discussed in the context of prayer. The fast puts the body and soul back into a right relationship. What we do with our bodies affects our spiritual selves, as they are inherently connected. We are not ghosts in a machine!

Fasting helps us align ourselves, body, mind, and spirit, with God's purpose in a way that transcends our cultural predispositions and connects us to something timeless, in much the same way as does our prayer life. As the Lord said, it is not what goes into a man that defiles him, but what comes out (Matt. 15:11). Many modern Christians interpret that to mean they can ignore the intake aspect, thinking that only what comes out is important. But, as a priest once asked me, how can we control what comes out if we cannot control what goes in? If we lack the discipline to follow simple commands, how can we master the truly difficult ones?

The Church, in giving us a fast, is actually giving us an easier exercise than the daunting task of immediately conquering something like anger. Fasting builds our spiritual muscles so we become able to conquer the tougher passions. To use an earlier analogy, someone who wants to run a marathon does not begin his training by running twenty-six miles. He begins incrementally, increasing the difficulty as he is able.

Fasting affords us a type of training tool, if you will, that enables us to see the connection between our physical and spiritual selves. For example, if a person comes to me and states that he struggles with lusting after women other than his wife, I do not simply say, "Stop being lustful." Given our fallen condition, that is like me telling him to climb Mt. Everest tomorrow!

Rather, I encourage people to increase their fasting discipline with the understanding that fasting and our struggle with sin are intimately connected. Our overindulgence in what goes into our bodies (something very common indeed in our modern culture) has a direct effect on our physical desires, and disciplining one aspect is made easier with the use of the tools given to us by the Church over the last two millennia. Trusting in this idea is difficult for many, because they see fasting as "legalistic" or something similar to what the Pharisees practiced. But that is a shortsighted view.

God doesn't legislate behavior. He gives freedom of choice and the option to *choose good*. In violating the fast given by Him, we open a door that progresses down a path. If we ignore the small things because of our modern understanding of legalism, we lose out on *why* these tools were prescribed—to aid in our path *toward* Christ, rather than away from Him.

To look at this from another angle, consider that the devil is, quite literally, "the divider" in that he wants to divide us from the truth. He divided Adam and Eve from the truth by twisting it, not in a way that seemed completely counter to what they understood, but rather in a manner that made sense. He separated them from the path toward God by convincing them they could figure it all out on their own.

Christ was unwilling to be separated from the truth, either in His humanity or in His divinity. When the devil presented Him with challenges similar to those of Adam and Eve, He was already relying on the *physical* tools God had given Him and not simply on an intellectual idea. He was in the wilderness and fasting; that is, He was removed from society and was disciplining His physical body in a way that kept Him on the path toward God rather than away from Him.

After Christ had fasted for forty days and nights, the devil told Him to turn stones into bread. Christ answered with a now-familiar phrase: "Man shall not live by bread alone, but by every word that proceeds from the mouth of God" (Deut. 8:3; Matt. 4:4). Whereas Adam chose earthly delights and his own path, Christ rebuked the devil by holding fast and returning to Scripture (Matt. 4:6–7). The text makes clear that His fasting was an integral part of His resolve.

It is interesting to consider at this point the great blessing God gave to humanity: freedom. Being made in God's image, humanity possesses freedom of choice. This is essential, for without freedom love is not possible. But freedom also introduces risk. The risk is that we might use our freedom wrongly. Saint Paul writes in 1 Corinthians 10:23, "All things are lawful for me, but not all things are helpful; all things are lawful for me, but not all things edify." It is true that we can do whatever we want, but doesn't our experience teach us that this is not beneficial?

In the Garden, Adam and Eve had the same freedom, and when God commanded them to fast, they were free to obey this commandment of God or disregard it. Using their freedom wrongly, they became self-directed, and this poor use of freedom led to their downfall. In like manner, Jesus was free to decide in the desert to fast or to eat. He freely decided to fast, and like the rest of His life and ministry, His fast healed the human condition of self-directed destruction.

This is why the Scriptures and the Church teach that fasting is not an optional spiritual discipline.

Notice that the Lord said *"when* you fast," not "if" (Matt. 6:16). Fasting is an integral part of walking as a Christian. But it is important to note that it is a commandment of *Christ*, not just an Old Testament law. If we wish for the Father, Son, and Holy Spirit to abide in us, we keep *His* commandments (John 14:15, 23).

Fasting quickens and clarifies the nous toward prayer in a way that little else does. Think of the lion who has just eaten a gazelle. He is not going anywhere—he's full! In order to be lifted up in prayer, we must be *light* in the spiritual sense—not weighed down or engorged by materiality.

We can look in other places to understand fasting in a different manner. During World War II, US Army supply lines for food had a difficult time keeping up with General George Patton's forces because he moved so fast. When he was informed of this problem, Patton famously replied, "My men can eat their belts, but my tanks gotta have gas."

While this may at first seem cruel, to deprive men of food instead of other supplies, Patton understood that a *hungry* army fought harder than one that was, as the saying goes, fat and happy. He knew that constant forward movement, even at the risk of being short on nourishment, was a far superior method of encountering the enemy than sitting and waiting for the stomachs of his men to be full.[11]

We can easily see how this applies to spiritual warfare. When we sit still and gorge ourselves, we lose sight of some of the most important aspects of our walk toward Christ.

Mark 9 contains a powerful passage that relates the healing of a father's son. The boy was often tormented, the text says, by a deaf and dumb spirit. "Wherever it seizes him, it throws him down; he foams at the mouth, gnashes his teeth, and becomes rigid" (Mark 9:18). The father brought the boy to the disciples of Christ, who were unable to help. Desperately he turned to Jesus for help. Jesus cast the spirit out of the boy and healed him. Afterward the disciples asked Jesus, "'Why could we not cast it out?' So He said to them, 'This kind can come out by nothing but prayer and fasting'" (Mark 9:28–29).

This passage of Scripture is read on the fourth Sunday of Great Lent. It connects spiritual warfare with the spiritual disciplines of prayer and fasting. While this connection is essential to our understanding of spiritual growth, we know that fasting is also connected to charity.

Fasting is intimately connected with charity

---

11 Victor Davis Hanson, *The Soul of Battle: From Ancient Times to the Present Day, How Three Great Liberators Vanquished Tyranny* (New York: Anchor Books, 2001).

in that what we *give up* should go to those in need, thereby creating a tangible result for our efforts. Saint John Chrysostom warned that fasting should lead one to be proficient in "charity, meekness, brotherly love,"[12] or it is of no use. It is important to recognize that these concepts are linked, as fasting from excess in order to give to others is a crucial part of spiritual discipline. Metropolitan Kallistos Ware tells us that "the second-century *Shepherd of Hermas* insists that the money saved through fasting is to be given to the widow, the orphan, and the poor"[13] as a way of reminding us that fasting has implications beyond our own development.

A great deal of spiritual discipline reflects and relates to our own will. To what is our will directed? In a lifestyle that is self-directed, our appetites become our masters, and we succumb to them.

We live in a time of extreme abundance, whether in terms of food, entertainment, or various other aspects of materiality, and it is easy to let our willpower guide us toward whatever feels right and

---

12   St. John Chrysostom, "The Homilies on the Gospel of St. Matthew," in A Select Library of the Nicene and Post-Nicene Fathers of the Christian Church, vol. 1, ed. Philip Schaaf (Veritatis Splendor Publications, 2012), Kindle edition.

13   Kallistos Ware and Mother Mary, "The True Nature of Fasting," Greek Orthodox Archdiocese of America, https://www.goarch.org/-/the-true-nature-of-fasting

good. If I hunger for anything, it is right there at my fingertips; my self-direction can satisfy that appetite with any number of immediately available options, leading me down a path of being a slave to those very cravings.

Fasting under the guidance of the Church offers us a way to break free of that self-conducted, self-inflicted enslavement to our physical appetites. In following the Church's guidelines and those of our spiritual father, we set aside our self-directed will and order our will rightly toward Christ. We fast as a *physical* way of submitting our desires to that which is holy.

Fasting does bring up an important question, however: Why did Adam and Eve need to fast in the Garden? If the Fall had not occurred yet, why did God prescribe a fast?

Think of it this way: all of our passions can be viewed as neutral. Our desires are not evil by nature; rather, the way we act on them can be beneficial or sinful. God created both Adam and Eve with the ability to *decide*; He simply offered them the same tools He offers us in aiding our decision-making.

We think of heaven in this way too—not as an end point where we stop growing, but as a place of infinite growth, because we can grow infinitely within God's infinitude. We move, as St. Paul tells us in 2 Corinthians 3:18, from "glory to glory" in a process the Church has always referred to as theosis. It is important to note, however, that our wills must reach a state of stability; theosis can only happen when the will is given a choice and chooses on its own, consistently, to do good.

Without fasting, we serve only ourselves, and our appetites become disordered; they become our masters. But if we keep the fast in the smallest way, we can, through Christ, begin to conquer the larger appetites of sinful behavior.

Is it possible for someone to go directly to the hardest spiritual disciplines? Could we just start out by conquering lust, pride, and anger? Theoretically, yes. But I would point out two very important facts: First, in all my years serving as a priest, I have never seen this happen. I have yet to witness an individual who does not benefit greatly from beginning with fasting or who can handle these monumental issues without the proper tools.

Second, and perhaps more important to the overall point, even the Lord did not start with the difficult things. When He went into the wilderness (*eremos* in Greek—a lonely and desolate place devoid of nourishment), He began with fasting and held to it while being tested. This is important, because it shows how God meets us and brings us life and nourishment in a place where they are absent, which is prefigured by Israel's time in the wilderness. He provided for them while they were there and then brought them out of it.

Christ then affirmed the importance of fasting in His command *"when* you fast," which interestingly comes in the middle of His Sermon on the Mount, immediately following a direction on *how to pray.*

These are all connected. Prayer, almsgiving, and fasting are integral parts of a Christian life. Yet we can go deeper still.

What does humankind do to survive? We take in fuel, some of which is good and some of which is not. Ancient Israel was given commands about which animals to eat and which to avoid, but those should be seen primarily in typological form. Swine, for example, are symbolic of human passions that are out of order (in the dirt and mire; of the world alone). The Israelites avoided pork as a prefiguring or typology of not being "earthly bound" (John 15:19; 17:14–16).

In Acts, God encourages Peter to preach the Good News to the Gentiles by way of a dream, which included a command to "kill and eat" animals that he considered "unclean." The voice told him, "What God has cleansed you must not call common" (Acts 10:10–16). If we view these words in light of church teaching, we understand that through Christ *all* has been made clean; He is that which sanctifies and makes holy. The fast of Israel was typological and preparatory—only fully understood through the work of Christ.

The idea of clean and unclean foods helps us discern what we consume with *all* of our senses. If we don't fast, if we do away with restraints on appetite, we follow the exact path of excessive self-indulgence and self-directed will that we are seeing right now in our world. Again, as St. Paul taught us, "All things are lawful for me, but not all things are helpful; all things are lawful for me, but not all things edify" (1 Cor. 10:23). For the Orthodox Christian, our concern is not a matter of one thing being lawful or permitted and another not; it is about what *edifies* and brings us closer to God. It is about freedom. We are not free if we are slaves to our appetites. Remember, Peter was freed to see these things *after* he submitted himself to the spiritual disciplines of fasting and prayer.

The problem with the secular approach to fasting is that it is self-serving. Bodily health is good, but in the eyes of the Church it is tangential to the ultimate goal, which is becoming closer to God. This is what we learn from Peter's vision: clarity about God's will is directly tied to spiritual disciplines that involve our physical selves. Matter matters!

Therefore, it is always of great importance to remember the ultimate goal of fasting and how we should align ourselves with it. It is easy to look at the practice as some sort of direct line to God, but this would be misguided and even dangerous to our spiritual health. Do not forget the words of one of the great saints: "Though fasting, prayer, almsgiving, temperance, and any other good thing whatever, be gathered together in you; without humility all fall away and perish."[14]

Different Types of Fasting

THE EUCHARISTIC FAST

THE CHURCH GIVES us different types of fasting. The most prevalent and important is the eucharistic fast.[15] Unlike most fasting in the Church, the eucharistic fast requires abstention from all food and drink before partaking of Communion. (Guidelines for the exact duration of this fast vary, but roughly we fast from the evening before a morning Liturgy or from breakfast or lunch before an evening one. Consult your parish priest for specifics.)

---

14   St. John Chrysostom, "Homily 15 on Matthew."
15   We also observe the seasonal fasts, like Great Lent, and the fast kept during the week on Wednesdays and Fridays. We have fasts related to special feasts and the potential for a prescribed fast for a specific person and a specific reason. Each fast has its own meaning, and, working together, they help us grow in our relationship and faithfulness to Christ.

To understand the origins of the eucharistic fast we have to turn to the New Testament. There we read that the disciples of Saint John the Baptist were fasting, and when they saw that the disciples of Christ were not, they inquired as to why. The Lord responded, "Can the friends of the bridegroom mourn as long as the bridegroom is with them? But the days will come when the bridegroom will be taken away from them, and then they will fast" (Matt. 9:15). The Church understands this text as a reference to the fast associated with receiving the Eucharist.

The meaning of this passage may not be immediately clear, but upon closer investigation we begin to see the connection. In the passage we cited, Jesus refers to Himself as a Bridegroom. This title is rich with symbolism. By using it Jesus reminds us that God's special relationship with us is like that of a groom to his bride. Weddings, as we know, are joyous occasions, and those who attend usually celebrate with a banquet the coming together of two people who have fallen in love with each other. Jesus is saying that His presence with His disciples is like the coming together of a groom with his bride, and it would be incongruous to fast in such a situation. Rather, the proper thing to do is to throw a feast, a party.

Conversely, Jesus in this same passage hints at His coming betrayal, arrest, and Passion, after which He will be crucified, rise from the dead, and then ascend into the heavens. To lose intimacy with one's beloved is a difficult thing. Today followers of Jesus live between these two realities, the presence of Christ and the absence of Christ. The eucharistic fast reminds us of what it would be like to be without our Bridegroom, Jesus. When we arrive at Church, we break this fast. Entering the banquet with our Bridegroom, we put away our sorrow over His absence from our lives as we receive Christ in the Holy Gifts of His Body and Blood.

Another way to look at this practice is to state that on Sunday, when we celebrate the Divine Liturgy, it is impossible for the followers of Jesus to fast because the Lord is with us through the Eucharist. We learn this from many places in the New Testament and in the writings of the early Church. However, one of the most powerful stories in the Gospel of Luke describes the presence of Christ in the Eucharist this way: Two disciples of Jesus were traveling, after the Lord's Crucifixion, from Jerusalem to Emmaus. While they were on their journey a third traveler, the Risen Christ, joined them. The Bible tells us that they began to converse with the Lord but did not yet recognize Him. "So it was, while they conversed and reasoned, that Jesus Himself drew near and went with them. But their eyes were restrained, so that they did not know Him" (Luke 24:15–16). In time these two disciples, Luke and Cleopas, reached their destination—an inn in the village of Emmaus. They still did not realize who they were talking with until this pivotal point in the story occurs.

> *Then they drew near to the village where they were going, and He indicated that He would have gone farther. But they constrained Him, saying, "Abide with us, for it is toward evening, and the day is far spent." And He went in to stay with them.*
>
> *Now it came to pass, as He sat at the table with them, that He took bread, blessed and broke it, and gave it to them. Then their eyes were opened and they knew Him; and He vanished from their sight. (Luke 24:28–31)*

Amazingly, the presence of the Risen Lord became known to the disciples of Jesus in the Eucharist. We know that Luke and Cleopas were so excited and transformed by this experience that they immediately left the inn, and returning from Emmaus to Jerusalem, they shared with the rest of the company of Jesus' disciples "how He was known to them in the breaking of the bread" (Luke 24:35). Each time we celebrate the Liturgy, we enter this mystery of the Emmaus supper. It is the meeting of heaven and earth, of you and me with the Divine. And though we commune and fast within the daily rhythm of life on earth, it is a feast outside of time, as the saints teach.[16]

A few last thoughts on this eucharistic fast are needed. Remember that Christ said, when tempted, that "man shall not live by bread alone." It is important to note here that the "daily bread" mentioned in the Lord's Prayer is beyond mere bread. The original Greek word that is normally translated as "daily" is *epiousious*—a word most scholars of Koine Greek agree would be better rendered as "supersubstantial." The Church has, for centuries, considered this word to be pointing to the Eucharist.

The intent here is not to delve deeply into eucharistic theology, but rather to indicate the importance of fasting *prior to* the Eucharist in an effort to rightly order ourselves before coming to the Lord's Table. We lighten our souls, as St. John Chrysostom said, so that we can be lifted up. Remember that what we do with our physical selves matters; worship is not just an idea in our heads. Communion, then, must involve more than thoughts. We commune most deeply with the Risen Lord—with the Bridegroom of our souls—by partaking of the Eucharist. In fasting beforehand, we recognize

---

16 The Church refers to the concept of time with two different terms—*chronos* and *kairos*. Whereas *chronos* is a linear description of time, *kairos* is immeasurable and ever-present.

the separation between us; in communing we realize the union. We fast because we, too, shall not live by mere bread alone, "but by every word that proceeds from the mouth of God."

THE FAST OF WEDNESDAYS AND FRIDAYS

IN DISCUSSING OUR prayer lives we mentioned an early Christian document, the *Didache*, that many scholars today connect with the first century. In it we learn about the Christian discipline of fasting on Wednesdays and Fridays (except in certain weeks, such as after Pascha). This weekly habit of fasting in the Church relates to spiritual disciplines. On Wednesday we commemorate the Lord's betrayal, on Friday His Crucifixion. This means that every week we commemorate the most important week in the history of humankind not only because it is important to us (though it most certainly is!), but also because it is the center of all history—it is the point in time from which all other events flow.

Every week we relive our story of redemption and learn how, through it, we transcend time with the meeting of heaven and earth. Again, when we do this, we incorporate our *whole selves*—mind, body, and spirit—in a manner guided by God's Word and His Holy Church. We do not invent our own method of fasting—not even Christ did that!

Above we mentioned that the eucharistic fast is a total fast from all food and drink. The fast we keep on Wednesday and Friday is not this type of fast. Rather, this fast is the sort many people are more accustomed to—a reduction in the type and amount of food we eat.

DETAILS OF FASTING

THIS IS PROBABLY a good point to discuss some of the rules of fasting. The amount of food we eat is as important as the type. In other words, if our fasting from meat means we simply feast on the finest caviar, we may have missed the point. While caviar is technically not a food to avoid during the fast, it is expensive, and gorging on it is not in the spirit of the fast. On fast days we should seek to simplify our diets and reduce our expense of time and money in preparing food. This provides us with more time and resources for charity and spiritual work. At the same time, we do consider the types of food we eat to be an important part of keeping the fast of the Church.

A basic rule of thumb is that fasting means we become vegans. While this rule may be difficult to follow for some, for others it is easy. Many in the Church are already vegans, and we need to consider how they might participate in the fast as well. We can address this issue by restricting the amount of food we eat.

Additionally, we should note that the simplicity of our food and its nutritional value are important. Preparing an exquisite dish of lentils and slaving over sauces and dips is a bit outside the point, as is eating Oreos, which technically meet the guidelines for fasting. At the same time, keeping the fast doesn't mean we should be eating only uncooked vegetables, although some have found this approach to be helpful. Regardless of our culinary approach, we should not miss the spirit of the fast while being obsessed with finding tasty ways to adhere to the letter of it.

It is beneficial to remember that we should not be public about our fasting or hold ourselves dourly to a rigid set of rules. Fasting is supposed to be a joyous means of developing our relationship with Christ. It is a discipline that lightens our spirits and focuses our hearts on living the gospel daily. Our Lord cautioned against fasting in a wrongheaded way:

When you fast, do not be like the hypocrites, with a sad countenance. For they disfigure their faces that they may appear to men to be fasting. Assuredly, I say to you, they have their reward. But you, when you fast, anoint your head and wash your face, so that you do not appear to men to be fasting, but to your Father who is in the secret place; and your Father who sees in secret will reward you openly. (Matt. 6:16–18)

Before we list some of the guidelines of fasting, it is important that we say a few more things by way of introduction. If we set too hard an edge around our fast and consider only the amount and type of foods and drinks we consume, we may miss one of fasting's great benefits—namely, freedom. If we take the time to examine ourselves, we quickly realize how attached we become to the things of this life. Some of these things are not evil or destructive, but, as the saying goes, too much of a good thing. If I love classical music and play it every day for hours on end, I may end up living a disfigured life.

Many of our attachments are less than beneficial. Who doesn't need to free themselves from their cell phones, from the screens that surround us, from attachments to entertainment, the news, or sports? If we simply keep the fast as prescribed by the Church but fail to address all aspects of our enslavement, we may never become free. I typically ask people to consider not only what they can fast from in terms of food and drink but to consider other aspects of their lives. It is a wonderful thing to gain one's freedom, as we discussed earlier, and then to put that freedom to use in a healthy and beneficial way. In doing this we can begin to think of fasting not as an experience of taking away but rather as a positive process that gives us back our freedom and our time to pursue true life.

In the rules of fasting, the Church teaches that we should fast from all meat—this includes poultry and pork as well as beef. Next, we fast from all dairy products—eggs as well. Then we eliminate fish from our diet, and finally alcohol and olive oil. We should note that the Church at times modifies the fasting rules. For instance, on some fast days fish is allowed, or wine and oil. It is helpful to note that if fish is allowed, this means wine and oil are okay as well. Or during the week of Cheesefare, prior to the start of Great Lent, dairy is allowed each day, and so are fish, wine, and oil. To help you know when the fast is kept and how, an Orthodox calendar is beneficial.

SEASONAL FASTS

IN ADDITION TO the eucharistic fast and the normal fasting cycle of Wednesdays and Fridays throughout the year, the Church encourages us to participate in different seasonal fasts. These all have their place in the Church and the rhythm of the calendar.

Four Major Fasts

GREAT LENT (MOST IMPORTANT)

OF ALL THE fasting periods, Great Lent is the most well known and recognized. Great Lent is a forty-day period of intense fasting (as well as prayer and almsgiving) leading up to the celebration of our Lord's Resurrection at Pascha. It is a period of self-examination and evaluation in which fasting is not an end in itself, but rather a means toward a greater goal, the Kingdom of God.

Great Lent went through a period of development that included the opportunity to initiate neophytes into the Christian life. It was the final preparation for their baptism and a way of participating within the community. Great Lent moved catechumens beyond just reading and contemplating into *living* in action within the Christian community. In time, this period of final preparation came to include those who had already joined the Church through baptism. While the preparation of people about to enter the Body of Christ still occurs during Great Lent, the season has become a time for renewing everyone's baptismal commitment as well.

The week leading up to Lent, Great Lent itself, and Holy Week take up a third of the Church year, so ignoring the Church's rhythm of fasting is detrimental to the renewal of the human person. The Great Lenten season is one of the most significant tools the Church has used to kindle or rekindle the hearts of the faithful toward Christ. It is also the most robust period of fasting.

The typology of the forty-day period is obvious from Scripture. When Noah and his family entered the ark, the rains fell for forty days; Moses fasted for forty days before receiving the Ten Commandments; Christ fasted for forty days in the desert after His Baptism; and Christ taught for forty days following His Resurrection, prior to His Ascension. The Scripture contains numerous examples of a period of forty days having great significance.

Interestingly, although modern studies show that the time required to change a bad habit into a good one can be slightly more or less than forty days, for thousands of years numerous cultures across the globe have seen this time period as significant.

All of us face the human experience of loss of focus and "going through the motions" in our daily routines. Lent shakes up those routines and brings back our focus. It gives us a tool for rightly ordering ourselves toward that which is holy and away from purely earthly norms.

A common response to Great Lent in some Christian circles is to say that all times are holy and that we should act righteously all the time—that the period of Lent should not be any better or more important than any other. But this view belies the human condition and what we learn from Holy Scripture as well—it loses sight of the idea of certain things being separate and sacred. No one actually lives as though every part of life were as sacred as all the rest.

God set up certain seasons and even places that are more holy than others. We see this as typology in the Old Testament and then see it lived out in the New by Christ and His apostles. Jesus Himself used a period of time (His forty days in the wilderness), and the apostles not only fasted but went out to set up churches and appointed others to do the same (Acts 13:3). If every place and every time is equally sacred, why start physical churches, and why fast? These practices have been the norm since the beginning of the Church.

The setting apart of times and places is also part of our everyday reality. No one acts as if every day is a birthday or Christmas. We recognize that there are special times, just as there are special places. You don't treat your garage the same as the church sanctuary—or at least I hope not!

During certain periods of time, the Christian's ability to focus on God grows. An understanding of the human condition is woven in here. We need these processes to build up our strength. When a professional athlete is preparing for an event, we understand that he cannot maintain that level of intense training indefinitely; it is for a certain purpose at a specific time, and that time is a season.

Great Lent is essentially the most robust reflection of this reality, that we need special seasons for rightly ordering our lives toward God. Fasting is an essential part of this right ordering, as it includes both our corporeal and spiritual selves to help us refocus and break from earthly routines.

THE DORMITION FAST
(SECOND MOST IMPORTANT)

THE DORMITION FAST begins on August 1 and ends with the Feast of the Dormition of the Mother of God on August 15.

We view Mary, the *Theotokos*,[17] as the first Christian, and an exceptional one. She was with Christ from His birth, all through His life, death, Resurrection, and Ascension—and her faith did not waver. She was the first to accept Him and the only one to witness His entire life. If being a Christian means being *with Christ*, no one did so better than Mary. She never departed from Him.

We also understand that she uses her particular position before the Lord as His Mother and disciple to intercede on our behalf. The supplicatory prayers

---

17 Translated as "Mother of God" or "God-bearer," *Theotokos* was a title given to Mary in the very early Church to affirm that she is the Mother of Christ, who is both God and man.

of a righteous man have much strength, St. James tells us (James 5:16). We also know that our God is the God of the living, and in the Gospel accounts of His Transfiguration we read that He consulted with both Elijah, who was taken alive to heaven, and Moses, who died before entering the Promised Land. In Christ, the Life-Giver, death is annihilated, and the living stand before His presence forever. We know that He honors His Mother and respects her intercessory efforts.

Mary stands before her Son and her God and continues to offer up her worthy prayers on our behalf. So, during the two weeks that precede the commemoration of her falling asleep on August 15, we pay special attention to her life and to her God-pleasing prayers. We supplicate her to intercede and pray for us, because she truly is a friend of humankind.

When new people come to the Orthodox Church, one of their biggest reservations relates to Mary and how she fits in with everything. She is, after all, a person who has been largely ignored in most modern Christian theology, yet she plays a prominent role in the worship and life of Orthodox Christianity. Without going into a major defense of Marian thought, I will offer just a few things to consider for those who find themselves with questions regarding Christ's Mother.

The first point to note is perhaps the most obvious, but it is often overlooked. When the Archangel Gabriel approaches Mary to announce Christ, his words are telling: "Rejoice, highly favored *one*, the Lord *is* with you; blessed *are* you among women!" (Luke 1:28).

When Gabriel appeared to Zacharias, he simply said, "Do not be afraid, Zacharias, for your prayer is heard; and your wife Elizabeth will bear you a son, and you shall call his name John" (Luke 1:13). Do you notice that Gabriel gives no title to Zacharias? The archangel does not address him specifically in any way, yet when he comes to Mary, the distinction is clear—*highly favored one*. Remember, angels are God's messengers and do not carry their own agendas. They do not say whatever they want to say. We should realize that Gabriel's greeting was the one God instructed him to use—this is what God Himself calls Mary.

Neither Joseph nor Zacharias receives an honorific title from the archangel, yet Mary does. This prompts the important question: Why should Christians not honor her in the same way?

Later in the same chapter, Mary states that "all generations shall call me blessed." This is exactly what the Orthodox Church does, and the Church pays special attention to her during the Dormition Fast. But keep in mind the name of the fast—*dormition* means literally "falling asleep," another way of referring to death. The Church is inviting each of us Christians to look at our own death. Christ's Mother died, so the Church is celebrating the faith of a human being who trusted that He would take care of her through death.

THE NATIVITY FAST
(LATER DEVELOPMENT)

THE NATIVITY FAST, like Great Lent, lasts for forty days, from November 15 until Christmas Eve. Although the feast of Christmas is widely accepted, a fast preceding it is not. The Nativity Fast has largely been ignored by modernity. The pre-Christmas season tends to be a time of parties and indulgence. So, inquirers often ask, why fast before the celebration of the Birth of our Lord?

Earlier in the chapter we discussed the concept of the Church calendar's rhythm and how it relates to God's design—how we are in harmony with His creation if we live within that rhythm. The fasting and feasting cycles of the Church are not only a manifestation of this harmony with creation, but they form a cornerstone of it as a foundational principle (along with prayer and almsgiving). Nowhere is the rhythm more physically *felt* than in fasting and feasting—especially in our culture!

To put this in practical terms, we simply point out that if the Church has a feast, rest assured that there will certainly be a fast preceding it. The Church recognizes that having one without the other leaves us out of balance and out of tune, so to speak, with the harmony God intended. Once again we can look here at the story of the Pharisees asking Christ why His disciples are not fasting, and the response He gives. In Matthew 9:15 He says, "Can the friends of the bridegroom mourn as long as the bridegroom is with them? But the days will come when the bridegroom will be taken away from them, and then they will fast." Christ is plainly showing that there are times to fast and times to feast—a natural rhythm, but one that is in accord with *Him*.

Have you ever noticed that food tastes even better after a fast? Have you ever been in a situation where you could not eat much food, or ate poor-quality food for an extended period of time? The first *real* meal you eat after that period is nothing short of amazing.

But we also know that if you ate nothing but amazing meals every time you were hungry, your definition of "amazing" would change; you would become jaded and gluttonous, experiencing nothing special. Fasting, in addition to having scientifically proven health benefits, helps put us back into a harmonious rhythm with God's will for His Church.

In other words, a feast without a fast runs decidedly counter to a proper balance. Celebrating Christ's Incarnation would be incomplete without a preparatory fast in which we realign ourselves with Him and His Church. So, much like the other fasts mentioned, we should approach the Nativity Fast with that principle in mind—a right ordering of ourselves with His will.

THE FAST OF THE APOSTLES
(FOURTH MOST IMPORTANT)

BEGINNING ON A Monday eight days after Pentecost and ending with the Feast of Saints Peter and Paul (June 29), the Fast of the Apostles may be one of the least known of the fasts, but it is also deeply rooted in Christian history and tradition.

Forty days after Christ's Resurrection, He was "taken up" and out of the sight of the apostles (Acts 1:9). In the period following His Ascension, the apostles "continued with one accord in prayer and supplication" (Acts 1:14). The Fast of the Apostles is a commemoration of this very time—we recognize Christ's Ascension and bestowing of the Holy Spirit on His Church as well as the importance of the work done by the apostles, to whom we owe so much. This season was the beginning of His Church, and it deserves remembering.

The fast ends with the Feast of Saints Peter and Paul—a celebration of the unity of two men with differences who still focused on what was most important. In the Epistle to the Galatians (2:11), we see evidence of a disagreement between Paul and Peter, with the former rebuking the latter regarding his view of how Gentiles and Jews should behave in accordance with the Law.

While hundreds of thousands of words have been written about this disagreement and its theological implications, what is important to recognize in the context of the Feast of Saints Peter and Paul is that they *resolved* their dispute—and laid the foundations for Christ's Church. They came together in unity rather than creating a schism. We celebrate that unity, but prior to the celebration we fast in remembrance and recognition of the incredible work they did.

Minor Fasts and Additional Thoughts on Our Weekly Fast

IN ADDITION TO the types of fasting mentioned above, we observe minor fast days[18] and individual fasts specifically prescribed by a spiritual father

---

18 Many minor fast days appear throughout the calendar year. Again, an Orthodox calendar is helpful in understanding when and where they fall.

based on one's own needs.[19] Both of these require a brief explanation but will enlighten our approach to fasting as a whole.

With the weekly fasts, remember that the Orthodox Church views *every* week as a mini-Pascha. Pascha is at the center of everything—not just time and space in a spiritual sense, but also in our weekly cycle.

When I was growing up, my grandmother did not always refer to days of the week as "Wednesday" or "Friday," but rather as days in relation to the Lord's day, *Kyriaki* (Sunday). In fact, this is how the Greek language refers to the days of the week. Monday, for example is known as "second day," the day after the day of days, the Lord's day, what we call Sunday. Her week, much like the cycle of the Church, was marked out by the liturgical calendar with the recognition of Pascha as the focal point of everything.

Although it is beyond the scope of this book to examine the reasons living in this weekly cycle fell out of favor, it is important to understand that it *did*. So, although fasting may be at odds with society as a whole today, it is, in fact, rightly ordered with historical Christianity.

The fact that fasting is so out of step with modernity, however, offers us a chance to examine how it

---

19   It is not unusual for a spiritual father to assign an individual fast to a Christian who is struggling with a specific sin.

relates to the individual in special circumstances. I am often questioned about this issue. Given that regular fasting is so alien to our culture, and that many are unaccustomed to it as a regular practice, the Church must understand this and act accordingly.

When encountering the fasting recommendations of the Church, many see them as "rules" and immediately become uncomfortable, often asking questions that start with a form of, "But what about . . ." What typically follows that phrase is something to do with the health or unique situation of an individual that makes it especially hard for her to follow the fast in its entirety.

In counseling those with such questions, I begin by relating the story about Jesus recorded in John 8, in which the Pharisees "brought to Him a woman caught in adultery" (8:3). They point out that, according to the Law, the woman should be stoned.

Christians often quote His response but rarely understand it to its full extent: "He who is without sin among you, let him throw a stone at her first" (8:7). What we have here is a look at the *oikonomia* of God working in relationship with His *akrivia*.

Akrivia is the precision or exactness of the Law; it is the strictest application of the Law of God. *Oikonomia*, on the other hand, is translated as "household management" but refers to the application of God's

Law with mercy to individual circumstances. In the above example, the akrivia of God's Law was that the woman should be stoned, but Christ applied oikonomia—grace and mercy worked out to the individual in a specific situation.

We can learn two lessons from this story. First, note that after her accusers departed, Christ did not tell the woman to continue as she was, living in the same manner. Rather, the Lord told her to "go and sin no more" (8:11). Oikonomia is not license to continue a life of sinful behavior because grace allows it, but a recognition of our situation and a working of grace within it for the purpose of bringing us closer to God, or rightly ordering our lives.

Second, it is highly important to our subject of fasting here to recognize that the woman did not apply oikonomia to herself of her own accord; Christ, who was physically present in her struggle, offered it to her. He recognized her situation, including the position of her accusers, and acted in relationship with her rather than simply applying the strictness of the Law.

To put this in a practical context for our era, imagine that a doctor prescribes you medicine for a specific ailment, but the medicine is to be taken three times daily with food. Despite the guidelines of fasting, the Church is not going to tell you to ignore your doctor's instructions just so you can keep the fast. As a priest, it is my vocation to recognize the specifics of the lives of my parishioners and act in relationship with them, based on the teachings of the Church.

Similarly, on a broader scale, the Orthodox Church here in America recognizes that fasting is more difficult due to the fact that it is not a cultural reality here as it is in countries where Orthodoxy is the norm. Restaurants here often do not have fast-friendly menu options; American culture as a whole is geared toward having the ability to consume whatever food you want whenever you want, which makes periods of fasting all the more difficult.

The Church understands this reality and works *with* individuals to understand their place in this struggle. But, again, this is why I stress the importance of having a spiritual father. These concepts cannot be regularly self-applied—they should come through the pastoral office. The Church, through love, looks at the circumstances of the person and modifies what is necessary.

The importance of fasting has largely been lost to modern culture, even within Christian circles, which is unfortunate because of what it offers in terms of spiritual growth. The relationship of personal issues to church teaching can be seen clearly through the practice of fasting, as it offers a tangible, active tool for understanding spiritual discipline and humility. If fasting is understood and applied through loving means, the potential for growth in these areas is tremendous.

Closing Thoughts

AS A FINAL note, I find it interesting how much of this attention to fasting has been lost despite its centrality to the Christian life. In other words, not until very recently (in historical terms) did Christians see fasting as something to be understood only in a "spiritual" (that is, nonphysical) context—despite the fact that the earliest Christian writings we possess affirm fasting as essential.

In the story of Creation, man's diet was vegetarian. Not until after the Fall did man eat animal flesh. God's intent for us was to eat a vegetarian diet. So, when we fast in the Church, we return to that ideal. Fasting is an appreciation for the material world God created while lessening our physical footprint on it. I say it over and over again, but it is worth repeating— matter matters!

Our physical nature is important in our relationship with God. Fasting from food and not being a slave to our appetites are disciplines that should not—or cannot—be ignored in our spiritual development. If people believe they can simply grow without fasting and that their spiritual selves are wholly independent from their physical bodies, they are, quite literally, trusting in a philosophy that even the Lord Jesus Christ Himself did not adhere to.

Follow the fasting recommendations of the Church and your spiritual father—along with understanding and participating in the Church's prayer and almsgiving prescriptions—for a *complete* approach to transform your life in Christ. Ignoring any one of these will, without question, result in an imbalance in yourself and those around you.

Conclusion

"But I say to you who hear, love your enemies, do good to those who hate you, bless those who curse you, pray for those who mistreat you. Whoever hits you on the cheek, offer him the other also; and whoever takes away your coat, do not withhold your shirt from him either. Give to everyone who asks of you, and whoever takes away what is yours, do not demand it back. Treat others the same way you want them to treat you. If you love those who love you, what credit is that to you? For even sinners love those who love them. If you do good to those who do good to you, what credit is that to you? For even sinners do the same. If you lend to those from whom you expect to receive, what credit is that to you? Even sinners lend to sinners in order to receive back the same amount. But love your enemies, and do good, and lend, expecting nothing in return; and your reward will be great, and you will be sons of the Most High; for He Himself is kind to ungrateful and evil men. Be merciful, just as your Father is merciful.

"Do not judge, and you will not be judged; and do not condemn, and you will not be condemned; pardon, and you will be pardoned. Give, and it will be given to you. They will pour into your lap a good measure— pressed down, shaken together, and running over. For by your standard of measure it will be measured to you in return." (Luke 6:27–37)

A GREAT MANY members of the community I am honored to serve come from varied backgrounds. They tell me of the mountains of literature they have read and the paths they have walked in an attempt to make sense of the life they have been given. Like all of us, they wish to be transformed and acquire the peace that comes from living a life in Christ, according to His teachings. In the quotation from Holy Scripture above we hear our Lord, in the Sermon on the Plain, paint a picture of what Christian life should look like. His description is challenging and inspiring, and it is amazing to consider what is possible when we have refashioned ourselves through prayer, almsgiving, and fasting. In such a state, loving an enemy and being merciful are not impossibilities but rather the actions and attitudes of one devoted to God.

What I have attempted to offer here is a simple starting point for addressing that very desire to walk with Christ and become like Christ—by simplifying the Church's teachings since the time of the apostles as they relate to the three-legged stool of spirituality. What we find is that the wisdom of the Orthodox Church is timeless, and if we ignore it then we do so to our detriment. Scripture and the Holy Fathers have given us what we need; we only need to choose to follow it.

But I feel compelled to close with a few important thoughts. First and foremost, although I have mentioned this more than once in this book, I would be remiss if I did not once again stress the importance of undertaking the prescriptions offered here *within the Church*—or, at the very least, under the direction of a spiritual father who is in the Church. While following a rule of prayer, almsgiving, and fasting on your own is certainly better than living completely outside of the Faith, we will never fully realize the richness of Christianity when our lives are self-directed.

We live in a gnostic, *me*-driven society. From shopping to voting to choosing a church, modern living is heavily focused on meeting individual needs, so our natural inclination is to take these things upon ourselves and pick and choose what works for us and what doesn't. Yet this is not the way Christ taught His disciples, nor is it the way they taught the men and women who followed them.

From the earliest times, we know that Christianity

was communal in nature, and the Fathers thought of the Church as something *real*—not an invisible concept that rests solely in our heads. The Church has physical structure and an ordered hierarchy that offers us salvific methods for reorienting our lives toward Christ our God. When we ignore this and try to live a knowledge-based faith that depends only on what is inside our own heads, we eventually hurt not only the community we could be a part of, but also ourselves, as we can never achieve our real potential by operating on our own. This is what the Scriptures teach, and this is what the Church Fathers taught. We would do well to remember that.

My second point ties into this principle: While each person has individual concerns, deciding the answers on our own is a dangerous path to follow. Remember our discussion on oikonomia and akrivia? We can find numerous scriptural references for how the grace of God was applied, seemingly outside the rules, for an individual. But when we do this with our own discretion, our tendency is to apply these graces to ourselves incorrectly.

I have on many occasions given advice to my parishioners to adjust their fasting or prayer rule to meet certain personal needs. Perhaps they have health conditions that, as per doctor's advice, do not allow them to fast prior to Liturgy on Sunday mornings, and this is completely fine. But this accommodation takes place *within the Church,* and only after we have built a relationship that helps me to understand the person—to include what is most important for him or her and where we can apply oikonomia within the context of being rightly ordered.

Note well that this right ordering does not happen based on the whims of individual desires, but in concert with scriptural teachings as handed down by apostolic succession all the way to my bishop, with whom I remain in frequent communication, and then to me. I do not, in other words, offer up a simple prayer and go where I feel my heart is leading me; I consult and learn from my bishop, my spiritual father, and the teachings of Scripture *through the Church* and her Holy Fathers.

None of us can do this on our own.

The three principles of prayer, almsgiving, and fasting given here remind us of this profound reality—we are not alone in this, and isolation only leads to misguided efforts, self-direction, and even despondency and spiritual poverty. But engaging in each of these disciplines within the Church and under the direction of a spiritual father offers us more than just *knowledge* of how to draw closer to Christ; it offers us a fully developed *physical* method for doing so.

Through following a prayer ritual as described

in these pages, we connect to timeless principles espoused by those who wrote Scripture and those who canonized it while also recognizing our communal nature and our true human nature—that of *anthropos*. We are sacramental beings before anything else, and living a sacramental life is heavily dependent on prayer of that nature—that is to say, prayer that is both sacramental and communal. Extemporaneous and spontaneous prayer invented from the heart may not be wrong, per se, but it can never replace the method prescribed by Scripture and the Church.

Almsgiving reminds us that what we materially own is not truly ours but belongs to Christ, and He commands us numerous times to share what we have with those less fortunate. Attempting to be a Christian without giving charitably to others is like trying to be a human being without breathing! We can also see numerous ways to give—not just monetary wealth, but our time and talents as well—but giving is unquestionably necessary.

And finally, we learned that fasting, although largely ignored by modernity and its excesses, is crucial to the development of a spiritual life. It is fascinating that modern science is, in many regards, ahead of a great many Christians on this subject, as fasting has been the teaching of the Church since the very beginning and the teaching of the Most Holy for even longer. What we put into our mouths matters, as we have seen, and it affects how we think, what we say, and what we do. Our discipline in this arena is perhaps more important now than ever.

I do hope you find what is written in these pages to be useful in your spiritual growth and that your path is either already connected to the Church or will be soon. What we do matters. Our physical actions, our giving of alms, and the way we treat our bodies affect not just our own lives, but the lives of those around us.[20] Our physical reality is important, because it is deeply connected to the spiritual.

---

20 See Elder Thaddeus of Vitovnica, *Our Thoughts Determine Our Lives: The Life and Teachings of Elder Thaddeus of Vitovnica* (Platina, CA: St. Herman of Alaska Brotherhood, 2009).

For Further Exploration

On Prayer

Bloom, Metropolitan Anthony. *Beginning to Pray.* New York: Paulist Press, 1970.

Brianchaninov, St. Ignatius. *The Field: Cultivating Salvation.* Translated by Nicholas Kotar. Jordanville, NY: The Printshop of St. Job of Pochaev, 2016.

Archimandrite Irenei. *The Beginnings of a Life of Prayer.* Platina, CA: St. Herman of Alaska Brotherhood, 2012.

PRAYER BOOKS

The Ancient Faith Prayer Book. Chesterton, IN: Ancient Faith Publishing, 2014.
This and a wide variety of other prayer books are available at www.store.ancientfaith.com.

On Almsgiving

Chrysostom, St. John, and John Henebry. *St. John Chrysostom on Repentance and Almsgiving,* The Fathers of the Church. Translated by Gus George Christo. Washington, DC: Catholic University of America Press, 1997.

Lloyd-Moffett, Stephen R. *Beauty for Ashes: The Spiritual Transformation of a Modern Greek Community.* Yonkers, NY: St Vladimir's Seminary Press, 2009.

White, Michael, and Tom Corcoran. *Rebuilt: Awakening the Faithful, Reaching the Lost, and Making Church Matter.* Notre Dame, IN: Ave Maria Press, 2013.

On Fasting

Madden, Rita. *Food, Faith, and Fasting: A Sacred Journey to Better Health.* Chesterton, IN: Ancient Faith Publishing, 2015.

Mandell, Catherine. *When You Fast: Recipes for Lenten Seasons.* Yonkers, NY: St Vladimir's Seminary Press, 2005.

Ware, Metropolitan Kallistos. "When You Fast" (Topical Series booklet). Chesterton, IN: Ancient Faith Publishing.

FATHER EVAN IS a parish priest in Colorado, where he has served for over eighteen years. In 2002, he founded the St. Nektarios Education Fund, a nonprofit student education program. The fund has established five schools in Africa, educating more than 5,000 students. Father Evan has directed summer camps, served on national boards, and hosts a live call-in radio show on Ancient Faith Radio, *Orthodoxy Live*. He speaks around the country on various topics. Father Evan and his wife, Presbytera Anastasia, are the happy parents of four, Alexia, Eleni, Maria, and Spyridon. They live in beautiful Fort Collins, Colorado, where they ski, fly fish, and hike.

Ancient Faith Publishing hopes you have enjoyed and benefited from this book. The proceeds from the sales of our books only partially cover the costs of operating our nonprofit ministry—which includes both the work of **Ancient Faith Publishing** and the work of **Ancient Faith Radio**. Your financial support makes it possible to continue this ministry both in print and online. Donations are tax-deductible and can be made at **www.ancientfaith.com.**

To view our other publications,
please visit our website: **store.ancientfaith.com**

 ANCIENT FAITH RADIO

Bringing you Orthodox Christian music,
readings, prayers, teaching, and podcasts
24 hours a day since 2004 at
www.ancientfaith.com